conversational canvas

Designing UX for Voice and Chat

william webb

contents

1 /
introduction to user experience (ux)

defining user experience (ux)

WELCOME, fellow tech enthusiasts, to the exciting world of User Experience or UX. If you're here, you might be pondering, "What exactly is UX?" An excellent question indeed, and by the time we complete this section, you will not only understand what UX is, but you'll also appreciate why it's pivotal in our tech-driven lives.

Think of your favorite restaurant for a moment. What makes it your top choice? Is it just the food, or is it also the friendly service, the ambiance, the ease of getting a reservation, or even the music they play? All these aspects come together to create a dining experience that you enjoy. Similarly, UX is all about the overall experience a user has while interacting with a digital product, be it a website, mobile app, software, or a digital service.

At the heart of UX is a simple question: "How does using this product make the user feel?" A product with good UX is not just functional and easy to use, but it also creates positive emotions, making users want to return.

However, UX isn't just about pretty graphics and aesthetics, although those are important too. UX encompasses all aspects of a product that a user interacts with. This includes user interface design, interaction design, information architecture, accessibility, and even services like customer support.

Let's delve a little deeper. A significant component of UX is usability, or in other words, how easy a product is to use. If a user struggles to navigate a website or can't figure out how to use an app, then the UX isn't doing its job. A product with excellent usability allows users to effortlessly accomplish their tasks, leading to a satisfying user experience.

Accessibility is another key aspect of UX. A good UX design ensures that everyone, including people with disabilities, can use the product. This could mean offering text descriptions for images for those who can't see them, providing subtitles for those who can't hear a video, or ensuring that all functions can be accessed using only a keyboard for those who can't use a mouse.

Another crucial part of UX is the user journey, which is the path a user takes when interacting with a product. A well-designed user journey guides the user to accomplish their goal, whether that's buying a product, finding information, or enjoying a game. The user journey should be seamless and intuitive, leading the user from one step to the next without confusion or frustration.

UX also involves a deep understanding of the user's needs and wants. This is usually achieved through a process called user research, which involves techniques like surveys, interviews, and user testing. The insights gained from user research help UX designers create products that truly resonate with users.

Now, you might ask, "Why is UX important?" The answer is simple: in the digital age, users have a multitude of options for any given product or service. If a user finds a website or app difficult to use, unattractive, or frustrating, they can easily switch to a competitor. By investing in UX, companies can ensure that users not only use their product but also enjoy the experience, leading to increased user engagement, brand loyalty, and ultimately, business success.

UX isn't just a part of the product design process; it's a

mindset. It's about putting users at the center of the design process and creating products that enrich their lives. It's about understanding that every detail, no matter how small, contributes to the overall user experience. And most importantly, it's about recognizing that good design is not just about how a product looks, but how it works.

Now that we've laid the foundation of understanding what UX is, we are ready to explore more intricate details of how it influences various aspects of our digital interaction. We will journey through the fascinating landscape of chat and voice UX, unravel the role of UX in shaping technology's future, and perhaps, prepare you for an exciting career in UX design. We're just getting started, so strap in and get ready for a fantastic ride into the captivating world of User Experience!

importance of ux in tech

Now that we've explored the fascinating world of User Experience, or UX, let's delve into why it's such an essential aspect in the realm of technology.

Have you ever stopped to wonder why you prefer certain websites, apps, or software over others? Perhaps it's the ease of navigation, the intuitive layout, or the simple joy you experience when interacting with the platform. At the core of these preferences is UX.

User Experience is not just about making a product usable; it's about making the product enjoyable and efficient for its intended users. Tech products are all about solving problems, and UX plays a crucial role in ensuring that these solutions are not only effective but also pleasant and engaging.

In a world where new technologies, apps, and platforms are being launched every day, standing out in the crowd can be challenging. A well-designed UX gives a product the competitive edge it needs. No matter how innovative or technologically advanced a product is, it won't achieve its full potential if users find it difficult or frustrating to use.

Think about any popular tech product that you use daily - a smartphone, a fitness tracker, or a digital assistant. What makes these products successful isn't just their functionality, but the fact that they're designed with the user's needs and experiences in mind.

UX also plays a vital role in building trust and loyalty with users. When a product is easy to use, reliable, and enjoyable, users are more likely to return and recommend it to others. They also tend to be more forgiving of minor issues or bugs if they generally have a positive experience with the product. This connection between UX and user trust becomes even more critical when dealing with sensitive data or transactions, such as in banking or healthcare applications.

Another key aspect of UX in tech is its impact on productivity. Consider enterprise software, for example. When the UX is poorly designed, employees can struggle to perform their tasks efficiently, leading to decreased productivity. However, a software with an excellent UX can streamline tasks, reduce errors, and even make work more enjoyable, leading to increased productivity and morale.

The importance of UX extends beyond individual products to shape the overall strategy of tech companies. By adopting a user-centric approach, companies can ensure that they're creating products that truly meet the needs of their users, leading to higher user engagement, customer satisfaction, and ultimately, business success.

UX also has a significant social impact. By considering accessibility and inclusivity in their designs, UX designers can create products that are usable by people with various abilities, ages, and cultural backgrounds. This not only widens the reach of technology but also empowers individuals by providing them with tools and platforms that cater to their needs

evolution of ux design

To understand the journey of UX Design, we need to wind back the clock to a time when computers were the size of entire rooms. Back then, in the 1950s and 60s, the concept of user-friendliness was quite foreign. Computers were utilitarian tools, and their use was limited to trained operators who had the patience and expertise to handle their complexity.

However, the seeds of UX were sown in this era with pioneers like psychologist Donald Norman and engineer Douglas Engelbart. They realized that to expand the benefits of technology, the design focus needed to shift from the machine to the human user. Engelbart, in particular, is renowned for inventing the mouse, a device that revolutionized human-computer interaction, making it more intuitive and user-friendly.

Fast forward to the 1980s, with the advent of personal computers like Apple's Macintosh. Tech companies began realizing the value of making their products more user-friendly. They started considering aspects such as usability and human factors in their design processes. However, the term 'User Experience' had not yet been coined. That credit goes to Donald Norman, who first used the term while working at Apple in the early 90s.

The 90s were also marked by the rise of the internet.

The introduction of the World Wide Web brought about new design challenges and opportunities. Now, not only did products need to be functional and user-friendly, but they also had to be navigable across an interconnected network. It was during this era that we saw the emergence of disciplines like Information Architecture and Interaction Design, both crucial components of modern UX Design.

The turn of the millennium brought with it the era of Web 2.0, characterized by increased user interactivity and the rise of social media platforms. The focus of UX Design expanded to include user engagement, community building, and content sharing. This period also saw a growing recognition of the value of good UX, with businesses starting to invest in dedicated UX roles and teams.

The next significant leap in the evolution of UX Design came with the explosion of smartphones and mobile apps. Suddenly, designers had to consider a whole new range of factors - smaller screens, touch interactions, location-based services, and more. This shift led to the advent of Mobile UX Design, a field dedicated to creating optimal user experiences on mobile devices.

Today, we are in the era of multi-platform, multi-device UX. Users expect seamless experiences as they switch between devices like smartphones, tablets, laptops, and even smartwatches. UX Designers now have to consider the entire user journey across multiple touchpoints, making the design process more complex yet more exciting than ever.

In recent years, we've also seen the rise of new technologies such as voice interfaces, virtual reality, and artificial intelligence, each bringing its own unique UX challenges and opportunities. These technologies are pushing the boundaries of UX Design, requiring designers to constantly learn and adapt.

Reflecting on this journey, we see that the evolution of UX Design is a story of increasing human-centricity in technology. From the era of room-sized computers to today's voice-enabled virtual assistants, the focus has consistently shifted towards creating more intuitive, engaging, and satisfying user experiences.

This evolution isn't just about technology, though. It's also a testament to our growing understanding of human psychology, needs, and behaviors. It's about recognizing that at the heart of every technology, every product, is a human user. As we look towards the future, this realization will continue to guide the growth of UX Design.

introduction to chat and voice ux

Now it's time to explore a fascinating aspect of the UX world that is rapidly gaining prominence - Chat and Voice UX.

But first, let's understand what we mean by Chat and Voice UX. Simply put, it's the field of UX design focused on creating effective and engaging user experiences for chat and voice interfaces. These could be chatbots on a website, voice-activated assistants like Amazon's Alexa, or even an interactive voice response (IVR) system on a customer service hotline.

Let's start with chat UX. A well-designed chat UX is all about creating a conversation with the user that feels natural, helpful, and engaging. It goes beyond just programming a bot to respond to specific commands. It involves understanding the user's needs and crafting responses that guide the user towards their goal, whether it's finding information, making a purchase, or getting support.

But designing a good chat UX is not without its challenges. A key one is maintaining the flow of the conversation. Just like in a real conversation, any sudden changes in topic or awkward pauses can confuse the user or make the conversation feel unnatural. It's also crucial to balance the need for efficiency (getting the user to their goal quickly) with the need for engagement (making the conversation enjoyable).

Now, let's move on to voice UX. As voice-activated technologies like smart speakers and voice assistants become increasingly popular, the need for good voice UX design is more crucial than ever.

A significant aspect of voice UX design is crafting effective voice prompts. These are the messages that the system speaks to guide the user. Good voice prompts are clear, concise, and anticipate the user's needs. For example, instead of saying "What can I help you with?" a more effective prompt could be "You can ask me about today's weather, news headlines, or set a reminder. What would you like to do?"

Another key consideration in voice UX is understanding and handling different user responses. Since voice interfaces allow for more free-form input than chat or graphical interfaces, the system must be prepared to handle a wide range of responses, including unexpected ones.

One of the challenges in designing voice UX is error handling. When the system doesn't understand the user's command, it should handle the error in a way that helps the user achieve their goal without causing frustration. This could involve asking clarifying questions, suggesting possible commands, or even employing a bit of humor to lighten the mood.

Both chat and voice UX require a deep understanding of the user's needs, contexts, and behaviors. For instance, a chatbot for a banking website would need to understand the types of queries and transactions users typically perform, while a voice assistant in a car would need to understand the user's needs and constraints while driving.

As we delve deeper into chat and voice UX in the upcoming sections, we'll uncover the strategies, best practices, and common pitfalls in designing for these interfaces. Whether you're a seasoned UX professional or a newcomer to the field, understanding chat and voice UX will equip you with the skills needed to create effective and engaging user experiences in this exciting era of conversational technology.

The journey into the world of User Experience continues to be as thrilling as ever. As we gear up to delve deeper into chat and voice UX, it's time to embrace the challenges and the learnings that lie ahead. Let's dive in!

2 /
understanding the users

identifying your audience

WE'VE EMBARKED on an intriguing journey, exploring the realms of User Experience (UX), its evolution, and the exciting world of chat and voice UX. Now, it's time to focus our attention on one of the most crucial aspects of UX design: Identifying your audience.

You see, creating exceptional user experiences begins with a deep understanding of who your users are. This is akin to a chef knowing their patrons' preferences to serve them dishes they will enjoy. As UX designers, our 'dishes' are the digital interfaces we craft, and our patrons are the users.

Identifying your audience is the process of under-standing and characterizing the users for whom you're designing. It involves understanding their needs, preferences, behaviors, constraints, and the context in which they'll be using the product. But how do we gather such insights? Let's explore.

The first step in this journey is User Research. This involves employing a variety of techniques to gather information about your users. Surveys, interviews, focus groups, observations, and user testing are all tools in the user researcher's kit. Each of these methods can offer valuable insights, but the key is to choose the right one based on your research goals, timeline, and resources.

Surveys and interviews can help understand users' attitudes, needs, and preferences. Observations and user testing, on the other hand, can reveal their behaviors, interaction patterns, and potential usability issues with your product. Focus groups can generate diverse ideas and opinions, though they may not provide in-depth individual insights.

Once you've gathered data about your users, the next step is to analyze this data to draw meaningful insights. Look for patterns and trends, such as common needs, recurring issues, or prevalent preferences. It's also essential to consider outliers - unique behaviors or needs that could indicate a niche audience or an unmet need.

These insights then feed into creating User

Personas. A persona is a fictional character that represents a segment of your users. It typically includes demographic information, behaviors, needs, goals, and even a fictional name and image. Personas help make the user 'real' for the design team, encouraging empathy and user-centric thinking.

But remember, identifying your audience isn't a one-time activity. As your product evolves and as you gather more data about your users, your understanding of your audience should also evolve. Regular user research and continuous feedback loops are essential to keep your design attuned to your users' changing needs and expectations.

In the context of chat and voice UX, understanding your audience takes on a whole new level of importance. Because these interfaces involve conversational interactions, the design must reflect the user's language, tone, and conversation style. Moreover, since voice and chat interfaces often lack the visual cues of graphical interfaces, they must be even more intuitive and user-friendly to ensure a smooth user experience.

As we continue our journey into the world of UX, the importance of identifying your audience will become increasingly clear. Whether we're exploring ethical considerations in UX, future trends, or practical tips and tricks, the user will remain at the heart of our discussions.

creating personas

Having learned about the importance of identifying our audience in the UX journey, we are now ready to delve into the next critical step: Creating Personas.

If we think about UX design as a story, personas are our main characters. They represent the people who will be interacting with our product, and the better we understand them, the better we can create experiences that they'll love and remember.

Creating personas starts with the user research data we have gathered. Whether through surveys, interviews, focus groups, or observations, this data forms the bedrock of our personas. It's like a treasure trove of insights about our users' behaviors, needs, preferences, and goals.

The first step in creating personas is to sift through our user data and identify patterns or trends. Perhaps we notice that many of our users share similar goals or face similar challenges. Maybe we see patterns in their behaviors or preferences. These commonalities help us identify different user groups within our broader audience.

Next, we give each group a face and a story by creating a persona. This persona should embody the key characteristics of the group it represents. It should have a name, a demographic profile, and a narrative that describes its behaviors, needs, and goals. It could also include other details such as lifestyle, occupation, technology usage, and even hobbies and interests, if relevant to our product.

Let's take an example. Suppose we are designing a chatbot for an online bookstore. Based on our research, we've identified a group of users who are avid readers, frequently buy books online, and value recommendations for new books. We could create a persona named "Rebecca," a 30-year-old lawyer who loves reading in her spare time and is always on the lookout for new books to read. She uses the chatbot to explore book recommendations based on her reading history.

A well-crafted persona like Rebecca allows us to step into our users' shoes and see our product from their perspective. It helps us understand what they might be thinking, feeling, and expecting when they interact with our product. This empathy is crucial for creating a user experience that truly resonates with our users.

Now, you might be wondering: How many personas should we create? Well, there's no one-size-fits-all answer. It depends on the diversity of your user base and the complexity of your product. But remember, the goal is not to create a persona for every individual user, but rather to represent the significant user groups within your audience.

One thing to keep in mind is that personas are not set in stone. As we gather more data about our users and as our product evolves, our personas should also evolve. Regularly revisiting and updating our personas helps ensure that our design remains user-centric.

Creating personas is a vital step in the UX design process. It helps ensure that our design decisions are grounded in a deep understanding of our users. It fosters empathy, facilitates collaboration, and keeps our focus squarely on the user throughout the design process.

In the chapters to come, we'll explore how these personas come into play as we delve into the nuts and bolts of chat and voice UX design. From crafting engaging dialogues to designing effective voice prompts, our personas will be our guides, ensuring that we never lose sight of the people at the heart of our design process.

user testing

User Testing, also known as Usability Testing, is the process of evaluating a product or service by testing it with representative users. This might bring to mind images of users huddled over a prototype while observers take diligent notes, and indeed, that is part of it. But user testing extends far beyond that scenario.

The process of user testing generally involves three key stages: planning, execution, and analysis.

In the planning stage, we define what we want to learn from the test. What questions do we want to answer? What parts of our design are we unsure about? What are our users' critical tasks, and how can we test them? We also need to decide who our test participants will be. Ideally, they should closely match our user personas.

Once we have a plan, we move on to the execution stage. Here, we ask our participants to perform tasks using our product, while we observe and record their interactions. This could be done in person or remotely, using a prototype or an actual product. It's important to note that we're not testing the users here; we're testing our design.

During the test, we want to capture as much as we can about the users' experience. What are they trying to achieve, and how successful are they? Where do they encounter difficulties? What do they like or dislike? Observing their actions, listening to their comments, and even noting their facial expressions and body language can all provide valuable insights.

Finally, in the analysis stage, we review our observations and findings. We look for trends, surprises, and especially for problems that users encountered. These insights feed back into our design process, helping us to refine our design and make it more user-friendly.

User testing is a powerful tool in the UX designer's toolkit, but it also presents some challenges. Recruiting representative users, planning and conducting tests, and interpreting the results all require time, resources, and expertise. But the insights and learning gained from user testing are well worth the investment.

In the context of chat and voice UX, user testing plays a crucial role. Because these interfaces are conversation-based, it's even more important to ensure that the interactions feel natural and intuitive to users. User testing can help identify issues such as misunderstood commands, unclear voice prompts, or conversation dead-ends that could frustrate users.

As we progress in our journey, we'll explore more about how to effectively conduct user testing for chat and voice UX. We'll delve into strategies for testing conversational flows, crafting effective test tasks, and analyzing user interactions. User testing, with its focus on real user feedback, will keep us grounded in our ultimate goal - creating user experiences that are not only functional but also delightful.

importance of cultural considerations

In an ever-globalizing world, the technology we create and the experiences we design are likely to reach beyond our own cultural boundaries. The products we create could be used by people from diverse cultures, languages, and backgrounds. This diversity enriches our world, but it also poses a significant challenge. How can we ensure that our designs are culturally sensitive and inclusive?

To answer this question, let's first consider what we mean by 'culture'. Culture is a complex tapestry woven with threads of language, traditions, beliefs, values, customs, and so much more. These cultural factors heavily influence how people perceive and interact with the world around them, including technology.

Thus, when we're designing UX for chat and voice, it becomes crucial to incorporate cultural considerations into our design process. We cannot assume that a design that works well in one culture will work just as effectively in another.

So how can we approach cultural considerations in UX design?

First, it begins with awareness. As designers, we must be aware of our own cultural biases and understand that our worldview is not universal. Being open-minded and willing to learn about other cultures is the first step towards creating culturally sensitive designs.

Second, it's essential to do our homework. Researching the cultures of our intended users can help us understand their preferences, values, and norms. This could involve reading up on cultural studies, consulting with cultural experts, or even conducting user research within those cultures.

Third, we need to think about localization, not just translation. If our product uses language, as in the case of chat and voice UX, it's not enough to just translate the words. We must also consider the context, the idioms, and the cultural nuances that come with language.

For instance, consider a voice assistant that uses humor in its responses. Humor can be a fantastic way to make interactions more engaging and delightful, but it's also highly culture-specific. A joke that's hilarious in one culture might be confusing or even offensive in another.

Finally, and perhaps most importantly, we must always approach cultural considerations with respect. Our goal should not be to stereotype or make assumptions about different cultures, but to understand and respect their diversity and uniqueness.

Cultural considerations in UX design can be a complex and challenging terrain to navigate, but it's a journey well worth undertaking. Designing with a cultural lens not only makes our products more inclusive and accessible but also enriches our understanding of the diverse world we live in.

As we move forward on our UX journey, let's carry the banner of cultural sensitivity high. Let's strive to create chat and voice experiences that celebrate diversity, foster inclusion, and respect cultural differences. By doing so, we'll be contributing to a more understanding, accepting, and connected global community.

Just as a landscape painter strives to capture the unique beauty of different terrains, let us as UX designers aspire to reflect the diverse cultures of our world in our designs. As we continue our journey, armed with the powerful tools of empathy, understanding, and respect, the world of UX design becomes a canvas for celebrating global diversity.

3 /
basics of chat ux design

conversational design principles

AS WE JOURNEY deeper into the fascinating world of UX design, our path now takes us to an area that's particularly relevant to chat and voice interfaces: the principles of conversational design.

In the realm of chat and voice UX, we're not just designing screens or pages; we're designing conversations. These are interactions that unfold over time, involving a back-and-forth exchange of information between the user and the system. Here, the user experience is defined by the quality of these conversations, making conversational design a cornerstone of chat and voice UX.

When designing a conversational interface, we are essentially crafting a personality, a tone of voice, and a communication style for our product. Hence, it's crucial to grasp the principles that guide conversational design. Let's delve into these principles that will help us shape engaging, efficient, and user-friendly conversational experiences.

1. Clarity and simplicity: The conversation with the user should be as clear and simple as possible. Keep in mind that you're designing for a wide range of users. Avoid jargon or complex language. Each interaction should make the user's path forward as clear as possible.

2. User-centric language: The language of your interface should revolve around the user. Use words and phrases that are familiar to them. This includes using the first person ("I", "me") when the system is talking about itself, and the second person ("you") when talking about the user.

3. Flexibility and forgiveness: People are unpredictable and might not always interact with your system in the ways you expect. Design your conversation to be flexible and forgiving. Allow for varied user inputs and have a system for handling unexpected responses.

4. Contextual understanding: A good conversation requires understanding the context. Remember past interactions and use them to inform the present

conversation. This helps in creating a seamless and personalized user experience.

5. Feedback and confirmation: Always let the user know that their input has been understood and processed. Provide feedback after each interaction. If a task takes time, use progress updates to keep the user informed.

6. Graceful error handling: Mistakes happen, and your system should be ready for them. Craft friendly, helpful error messages that guide the user back on track without making them feel bad for making a mistake.

7. Personality and tone: Your conversational interface isn't just a tool; it's a character that users interact with. Give it a personality that aligns with your brand and resonates with your users. The tone of the conversation should fit the context of the interaction and the user's emotional state.

Understanding these principles gives us the foundation needed to design effective chat and voice UX. But remember, principles are just guides, not hard and fast rules. The beauty of design lies in finding creative solutions within these guidelines that best serve our users' needs.

As we move ahead in our UX journey, these principles will be our trusty companions, guiding us in crafting engaging conversational experiences. With every conversation we design, we will be shaping inter-actions that not only meet our users' needs but also engage them in a meaningful and delightful dialogue.

Envision yourself not just as a UX designer but as a conversation architect, creating blueprints for exchanges that feel intuitive, respectful, and engaging. As we forge ahead, let's carry this vision with us, eager to design conversations that make our users' interactions with technology more human, more natural, and more enjoyable.

designing for text-based chat

Text-based chat interfaces, whether in the form of chat-bots or messaging apps, are becoming increasingly prevalent in today's digital landscape. These interfaces open a world of interactive possibilities, with the potential for dynamic, engaging, and personable exchanges that can greatly enhance a user's experience.

Designing for text-based chat isn't just about crafting visually pleasing interfaces. Rather, it's about orchestrating meaningful and fluid conversations. As we embark on this path, let's discuss some key factors that can guide us in creating user-centric and effective chat designs.

1. Understanding user needs: Designing a chat

interface begins by understanding who your users are and what they need. Conduct user research, create user personas, and map out user journeys. This will help you determine the style of conversation, the complexity of language, and the type of information your chat interface should handle.

2. Designing the conversation flow: Good chat design is about more than just exchanging messages. It's about facilitating a seamless conversation flow. Map out the likely paths a conversation can take, from initial greeting to concluding the interaction, and all the twists and turns in between.

3. Writing the script: Drafting a compelling and user-friendly script is crucial in chat design. Use clear, concise language. Make sure your chatbot's responses sound natural and human-like, without being overly robotic or impersonal. Remember, the objective is to foster a feeling of interaction and engagement.

4. Handling user inputs: Your chat interface should be capable of understanding and responding appropriately to various user inputs. Think about how you'll handle misspellings, slang, abbreviations, and other non-standard inputs. The more effectively you can manage different inputs, the better the user experience will be.

5. Managing errors and exceptions: Your chat interface should be designed to handle errors gracefully. If

the chatbot doesn't understand a user's input, it should guide the user back into the conversation flow without making them feel frustrated or confused.

6. Providing options and suggestions: One effective way to keep the conversation flowing smoothly is by providing users with quick replies or suggested responses. This can make the interaction more efficient and can guide users towards accomplishing their goals.

7. Making it visually appealing: Although the focus is on conversation, the visual design of your chat interface also plays an important role. Use color, typography, and layout to create an interface that's pleasing to the eye and easy to navigate. Make sure your design is consistent with your overall brand identity.

8. Including appropriate interactivity: Text-based chat doesn't mean you can't include other forms of interactivity. Depending on your user needs, you might incorporate images, emojis, links, or even small games within the chat.

Designing for text-based chat can be a thrilling journey. Each conversation your interface hosts is a chance to engage with a user, solve a problem, or provide a moment of delight. As we step into the realm of text-based chat, let's remember that we are not just building a tool, but we are also crafting an experience.

As we continue our journey through the world of UX, let's carry these insights with us. May they serve as a beacon, guiding us towards creating text-based chat designs that resonate with our users and bring a human touch to digital interactions.

creating chat flows

Chat flows are akin to the blueprint of a conversation, outlining the potential pathways a user can take when interacting with your chat interface. Just as an architect designs the flow of spaces in a building, we, as UX designers, are tasked with planning the flow of conversations in our chat interfaces.

Understanding and designing effective chat flows is a crucial step in crafting engaging and meaningful conversational experiences. So let's embark on this exciting journey and uncover the secrets of creating compelling chat flows.

1. Understanding the User's Goal: The first step in creating chat flows is to understand the user's goal. What is it that they're trying to achieve by engaging in a conversation with your chat interface? Whether it's getting information, making a purchase, or seeking support, clearly defining the user's goal will help you design a focused and effective chat flow.

2. Mapping the Conversation: Once you understand the user's goal, start mapping out the conversation. This involves envisioning the possible routes a user can

take to reach their desired outcome. Consider all the likely responses your chatbot will need to accommodate, along with potential deviations or exceptions that might occur.

3. Designing the Path: With the conversation mapped, begin designing the chat flow path. This is where you determine the sequence of questions and responses that guide the user towards their goal. Make sure your chat flow is logical and easy to follow, while also allowing for flexibility and spontaneity.

4. Creating Decision Points: Decision points are moments in the conversation where the user has to make a choice that will steer the course of the chat. These could involve choosing between multiple options or deciding whether to continue or end the conversation. Design these decision points carefully to ensure they enhance, rather than hinder, the user's journey.

5. Accounting for User Inputs: User inputs can greatly influence the course of the chat flow. As such, your chat flow should be capable of handling a variety of inputs - from straightforward responses to unexpected comments. Think about how you'll deal with misspellings, misunderstandings, and off-topic queries.

6. Incorporating Feedback and Confirmation: Part of creating a good chat flow involves letting the user know they're being understood. Include feedback and

confirmation in your chat flow to ensure the user knows their inputs have been processed and they're progressing towards their goal.

7. Planning for Errors: Errors are inevitable in any conversation. How you handle them can greatly influence the user's experience. Plan for error handling in your chat flow, ensuring the user is gently guided back on track if they veer off course.

8. Iterating and Refining: Finally, remember that designing chat flows is an iterative process. Based on user testing and feedback, you'll need to continually refine your chat flows to better meet your users' needs.

Creating chat flows is like choreographing a dance - it requires a careful balance of structure and spontaneity, logic and creativity. As you step into the role of a chat flow choreographer, remember that every conversation is an opportunity to guide, engage, and delight your users.

The challenge of designing chat flows is a thrilling one, and I'm confident you're up for it. With the insights we've gleaned thus far, let's leap into this new section of our UX journey, ready to craft chat flows that transform our users' interactions into memorable experiences.

the role of chatbots in ux

Chatbots, those AI-driven conversational agents, have emerged as potent tools in the UX designer's arsenal. They serve as intermediaries, facilitating interaction between users and digital platforms. Their role in transforming how users engage with online services is profound, reshaping the landscape of UX as we know it.

In this section, we will unearth the key facets of chatbots, exploring their roles and diving into how they influence and enhance user experiences.

1. Chatbots as Customer Service Representatives: Chatbots excel in customer service roles. They are available around the clock, able to handle multiple inquiries simultaneously, and respond in real-time, ensuring users get the help they need when they need it. This ease and immediacy significantly enhance the user experience.

2. Chatbots as Guides: Chatbots also serve as effective guides, leading users through complex processes, be it completing a purchase, booking a service, or navigating a platform. By providing step-by-step assistance, they simplify complex tasks and make the user's journey more comfortable and less daunting.

3. Personalization with Chatbots: Chatbots can offer personalized experiences based on user behavior, pref-

erences, and past interactions. This tailored approach results in more relevant and engaging interactions, strengthening the user's relationship with the platform.

4. Chatbots as Information Dispensers: Chatbots are equipped to provide users with pertinent information quickly and efficiently. Whether it's answering product queries, providing updates, or delivering news, they help users access the information they seek, enhancing the overall user experience.

5. Chatbots and User Engagement: Chatbots can play a key role in driving user engagement. By initiating conversations, recommending products, or offering interactive content, they can effectively engage users, prolonging their interaction with the platform.

6. Streamlining Processes with Chatbots: From gathering user information to handling transactions, chatbots can streamline various processes, making them more efficient and user-friendly. This not only saves time but also makes the user's journey smoother and more enjoyable.

7. Chatbots as Learning Tools: Chatbots can act as learning tools, educating users about various aspects of a platform or service. Through interactive tutorials and Q&A sessions, they can turn learning into an engaging experience

Chatbots, with their multifaceted roles and abilities, are revolutionizing the user experience. Their versatility, efficiency, and capability to provide personalized, real-time assistance make them invaluable in crafting meaningful and engaging UX.

As we venture further into the world of UX design, let's remember the significant role chatbots play and the profound impact they have on a user's digital journey. Equipped with this understanding, we can more effectively integrate them into our designs, leveraging their capabilities to enhance the user experience.

4 /
basics of voice ux design

how to talk like a person

ONE OF THE key facets of UX in chat and voice interfaces is their ability to mimic human conversation authentically. This human-like interaction not only builds user trust and engagement but also enhances the overall user experience. But how do we achieve this humanization of machine interactions? Let's dive into the techniques and strategies that will help us do just that.

1. Using Natural Language: One of the simplest ways to humanize chat interfaces is to use natural language. Avoid overly formal or technical language. Instead, opt for a conversational tone, using common phrases and expressions that users would encounter in their everyday conversations.

2. Emulating Emotion: While chatbots can't feel emotions, they can be programmed to understand and respond to them. Analyzing users' input for emotional cues and tailoring responses accordingly can make interactions feel more genuine and empathetic.

3. Personalization: Personalization can make a conversation feel more human. This can range from using the user's name to tailoring the conversation based on their past interactions, preferences, and behavior. A personalized interaction feels more like a conversation with a friend rather than a machine.

4. Adding a Dash of Humor: A little humor can go a long way in making chat interactions feel more human. When appropriate, adding light-hearted humor, puns, or witty responses can make the conversation more enjoyable and engaging for the user.

5. Contextual Awareness: Understanding and retaining context from past interactions is a crucial aspect of human conversation. Incorporating this feature into your chat interface can make conversations feel more coherent and natural.

6. Active Listening Indicators: In face-to-face conversations, we use nods and affirmations like "uh-huh" or "I see" to show we're listening. Chat interfaces can mimic this by providing feedback that shows they're "listening" and "understanding", such as "Got it" or "Let me see if I understand correctly…".

7. Variety in Responses: Humans rarely respond the same way to repeated stimuli. Incorporating a variety of responses for the same query can make your chat interface seem less robotic and more human-like.

8. Avoiding Over-Promising: It's important for chat interfaces to recognize and communicate their limitations to avoid creating false expectations. Being upfront about what the chat interface can and can't do can build trust and prevent user frustration.

9. Apologizing Gracefully: Mistakes are a part of being human. When the chat interface errs, acknowledging the mistake and apologizing can make the interaction feel more authentic.

Implementing these strategies can help your chat interface come across as more human-like, fostering a sense of familiarity and trust with users. As we design chat interfaces that talk like a person, we're not just making technology more accessible; we're also creating experiences that resonate on a more personal level with users.

creating complex conversations

Creating complex conversations means enabling our chat interfaces to handle more nuanced and intricate discussions, managing multiple topics, understanding indirect inquiries, and providing more thoughtful responses. This evolution of our interfaces can significantly enrich the user experience. Let's explore how we can make these complex conversations a reality.

1. Building in Contextual Understanding: We've already touched on the importance of contextual awareness, but in complex conversations, this becomes even more crucial. Our interfaces need to recall past interactions, understand the present context, and anticipate potential future queries. This could mean remembering user preferences, retaining data from past interactions, or even picking up cues from the current conversation to provide more thoughtful responses.

2. Branching Conversations: Conversations are rarely linear; they often branch out in multiple directions. Designing your interface to handle these branches smoothly can result in more engaging and lifelike interactions. This can be achieved by structuring your conversation design to accommodate tangents and ensure the user can return to the main conversation seamlessly.

3. Handling Indirect Queries: Humans often communicate their needs indirectly, and complex conversations should account for this. Enhance your interface's ability to understand and respond to these indirect queries by incorporating Natural Language Processing (NLP) techniques and a robust knowledge base that can infer the user's needs.

4. Providing Multi-faceted Responses: Complex conversations aren't just about understanding queries, but also about providing multi-faceted responses. These can include text responses, useful links, related suggestions, or even multimedia content, thereby enriching the conversation.

5. Integrating External Data Sources: To handle complex queries, your chat interface may need to pull in data from external sources. This could involve checking real-time data, accessing databases, or even interacting with other APIs. This level of integration can greatly increase the depth and complexity of the conversations your interface can handle.

6. Adding Predictive Capabilities: Using machine learning algorithms, your chat interface can learn from past interactions to predict and pre-empt user needs, adding a new layer of complexity to the conversation.

7. Designing for Empathy: Complex conversations involve empathetic responses. This could be as simple as expressing understanding when a user is frustrated or offering comforting words in a challenging situation. It's these human touches that make conversations truly complex and engaging.

Creating complex conversations is a challenging but rewarding process. It takes our chat interfaces from being simple tools to dynamic conversational partners, capable of providing rich and meaningful interactions.

how to build context into the conversation

After discussing how to create complex conversations, we now focus on one of the key components of those intricate discussions - context. Building context into conversations is like laying the foundation for a house. Without a strong foundation, the house won't stand; without context, conversations will lack depth and relevance.

First, let's define what we mean by 'context' in a conversation. It is essentially the background, the setting, or the situation in which the conversation takes place. In UX design for chat, context is what makes the interaction meaningful and personal for the user. Let's get started on how we can weave context into our conversations.

1. Remembering Past Interactions: A good starting point for building context is remembering past interactions. Imagine talking to a friend who forgets everything you've ever told them. Frustrating, right? That's how users feel when a chat interface doesn't remember past interactions. Make sure your interface keeps track of past conversations and preferences. This way, users won't need to repeat themselves, and the interface can provide personalized responses.

2. Understanding the Current Situation: Just as

important as recalling past interactions is understanding the current situation. If a user is booking a flight, your chat interface should understand that the conversation's context is travel. It should then provide relevant responses, such as suggesting hotels or offering travel tips. Use data from the ongoing conversation and other available sources to ensure your interface understands the context accurately.

3. Anticipating Future Needs: Building context also involves anticipating future needs. If a user has been researching smartphones, your interface can anticipate that they may be interested in phone accessories. Predictive analysis techniques can help your chat interface become proactive rather than reactive, improving the user experience.

4. Incorporating External Data: Incorporating external data can add another layer of context. For example, using data from the user's device, like location or time, can make conversations more relevant. If a user asks for restaurant suggestions, providing options based on their location enhances the interaction's context.

5. Leveraging User Profiles: User profiles are a treasure trove of contextual information. Details like age, interests, or past purchases can help customize conversations. The more you know about the user, the more context you can build into the conversation.

6. Recognizing Emotional Cues: Humans convey a lot of information through emotional cues. By identifying these cues in conversations, your chat interface can provide more empathetic and contextually appropriate responses. For instance, if a user expresses frustration, the interface could respond more sympathetically.

7. Using Natural Language Processing (NLP): NLP techniques can greatly enhance the contextual understanding of your chat interface. NLP can help understand the user's intent, extract relevant information, and provide more accurate responses.

Building context into conversations is no easy task, but it's well worth the effort. It leads to more engaging, meaningful, and personal interactions. Context is the secret ingredient that adds life to conversations, transforming them from mere exchanges of information into rich, satisfying interactions.

understanding voice technology

We're shifting gears in this section and turning our attention to a thrilling facet of UX design: voice technology. This fascinating area is revolutionizing how we interact with devices and bringing UX design into the realm of the spoken word. The voice is a powerful tool for communication, and it's time we fully understand it in a tech-savvy context.

Let's start at the beginning: what is voice technology? Simply put, it is technology that uses voice recognition, natural language processing, and speech synthesis to enable human-computer interactions based on voice commands. It's the technology behind the voices in your smartphones, smart speakers, and many other devices.

1. Voice Recognition: The first step in voice technology is voice recognition or speech recognition. This process involves converting spoken language into written text. This may sound simple, but remember, people have different accents, speech patterns, and even speech impediments. Voice recognition technology must account for these differences and understand spoken words accurately.

2. Natural Language Processing (NLP): Once the voice is converted into text, the next step is to make sense of it. That's where NLP comes in. NLP allows computers to understand, interpret, and respond to human language in a valuable way. It deals with the complexities of human language, including context, tone, and more. NLP is also the technology that allows your device to understand whether you are asking a question, giving a command, or making a request.

3. Speech Synthesis: Also known as text-to-speech,

this component of voice technology converts text data into spoken words. The aim is to make the computer-generated voice sound as human-like as possible, complete with appropriate pauses, intonation, and emphasis.

With these three pillars of voice technology, we can design experiences that understand, interpret, and respond to users. It's about creating an interface that feels natural and human, even though it's powered by lines of code and algorithms.

But why is understanding voice technology important for UX designers? Here's why: it opens up a world of possibilities for more intuitive, accessible, and efficient interactions. By leveraging voice technology, we can design experiences that are not confined to the limits of a screen. We can reach users who are visually impaired, occupied with tasks that keep their hands busy, or simply prefer speaking to typing.

Voice technology also brings a new level of personalization to UX design. Think about it: our voices carry a wealth of information, from our mood and intent to our identity. With voice technology, we can design experiences that listen to users (quite literally), understand them better, and respond in ways that are truly personalized.

However, designing for voice also comes with its

unique challenges. For one, it's a relatively new field, and best practices are still emerging. Also, designing for voice involves considering factors like speech patterns, accents, and cultural nuances. And let's not forget privacy concerns: as we invite technology to listen to us, we must ensure user's data is respected and protected.

As we delve deeper into this exciting realm, let's remember to approach it with curiosity and an open mind. Voice technology holds immense potential, and it's up to us UX designers to tap into it and create experiences that truly resonate with users.

designing for voice interfaces

Having developed a solid understanding of voice technology in the previous section, we're now primed to dive into the depths of designing for voice interfaces. These interfaces, driven by the natural ease of conversation, are poised to become a fundamental part of our technological future. By the end of this section, you'll be equipped with foundational knowledge and techniques to design a voice-first experience that is intuitive, responsive, and enjoyable for users.

Let's first recap what a voice interface is. A voice user interface (VUI) allows users to interact with a system through voice or speech commands. It's the technology that powers your digital assistants, like Siri, Alexa, or Google Assistant.

The first critical aspect of designing for voice interfaces is understanding the user's context. This involves considering where and when users will be interacting with your VUI. Will they be at home, at work, or in transit? Will they be multitasking? Knowing the context will help you design a VUI that can respond effectively to voice commands without disrupting the user's activities.

Next up is crafting a conversational flow. Unlike visual interfaces, where users can choose from visible options, VUIs rely on verbal instructions. Therefore, it's essential to design a logical and intuitive conversational flow. This includes defining the types of requests the system can handle, how the system should respond, and what happens if the system doesn't understand a command.

A successful VUI is a collaboration between the user and the system. It's essential to make users feel like they're having a real conversation. To do this, we need to design prompts that are clear, concise, and conversational. The system should also provide feedback to let the user know it's processing the request or if it needs more information.

In VUI design, error handling is of utmost importance. Errors in voice interfaces can be particularly frustrating because users cannot 'see' what went wrong. An effective VUI will anticipate errors and handle them gracefully, with clear instructions to guide the user back on track.

Another key consideration in VUI design is accessibility. Voice interfaces can be a boon for people with visual impairments, motor disabilities, or those who are not comfortable with traditional UIs. Therefore, it's crucial to ensure that your VUI is designed to be inclusive and accessible to all users.

Privacy is also a significant concern in VUI design. As designers, we have a responsibility to design systems that respect users' privacy and make it clear when and how their voice data is being used.

As you can see, designing for voice interfaces is not merely about the technology, but about understanding human communication, empathy, and respect for the user.

Even as we wrap up this section, remember that the field of VUI design is evolving rapidly, and new challenges and opportunities are emerging all the time. Stay curious, keep learning, and remember that at the heart of any successful VUI is a conversation that feels natural, helpful, and respectful.

voice flow and script development

By now, we have a pretty firm grasp of what voice user interfaces (VUIs) are and how they fit into the broader landscape of UX design. Now, let's explore the crucial stage of developing a voice flow and writing a script for our voice interfaces.

Imagine a VUI as a character in a play. How well the character is received depends on the script and how effectively it performs its role. In this section, we're going to learn how to be fantastic playwrights for our VUIs, ensuring they can deliver their lines effectively and respond appropriately to the user.

Let's begin with voice flow. Essentially, a voice flow is the map of a conversation between the user and the VUI. It shows the possible paths that a user can take to accomplish a specific goal. To create a voice flow, you need to understand the task your user is trying to accomplish and outline the possible interactions they might have with the VUI.

Start by sketching a basic flow of the conversation, including user commands and VUI responses. This initial sketch doesn't have to be perfect; it's more about exploring possibilities and getting a sense of the conversation's shape. From there, you can refine your flow, adding more complexity and alternative paths as needed.

An important part of designing voice flow is considering error paths. Unlike with graphical interfaces, where users can backtrack or select other visible options, VUIs need to handle errors in real time. Planning for these situations in your voice flow is vital to maintaining a smooth, user-friendly experience.

Next, let's discuss script development. If the voice flow is the map, the script is the journey itself. It's the language, phrases, and questions that the VUI will use to interact with users.

Scripting for VUIs is a fascinating challenge because it requires us to write for the spoken, not the written word. Conversations are dynamic and fluid, so your script should be too. Aim for natural language that mirrors how people speak in everyday life. Avoid complex sentences and technical jargon. Make your script conversational, friendly, and engaging.

Empathy plays a critical role in script writing. Remember, we're aiming for a dialogue that feels like it's between two humans, not a human and a machine. Think about how your user might feel at different points in the conversation and let that guide your script.

Iterative testing and refining are crucial in voice flow and script development. This process should be cyclical: design, test, refine, and then repeat. Use your findings from each test to improve the voice flow and script. Consider how users are interacting with your VUI, where they encounter difficulties, and how the script could be adjusted to improve the experience.

Keep in mind, it's not just what the VUI says, but how it says it. Tone, pace, and inflection can change the meaning of a phrase entirely. Consider the emotional context of your dialogue and adjust the VUI's tone accordingly.

Our journey through voice flow and script development may seem like an intricate dance, but it's an exciting part of creating VUIs. As we move forward, we'll learn to appreciate how this dance brings life to our voice interfaces, making them feel less like machines and more like friendly, helpful companions.

building voice user interfaces (vuis)

VUIs have an interesting characteristic that sets them apart from traditional graphical user interfaces (GUIs): they're invisible. While GUIs can use visuals like buttons and menus to guide users, VUIs have only their voice. This unique challenge is part of what makes building VUIs such a fascinating task.

To build effective VUIs, we need to start with a clear purpose. What tasks is our VUI going to help users complete? Will it help them order food, book a hotel, navigate a website, or perhaps something else entirely? Defining the purpose from the onset will help guide our design decisions.

Once we know the purpose of our VUI, we can begin designing the conversation. As we discussed in previous sections, we start with developing the voice flow and scripting the conversation. These steps form the backbone of our VUI, outlining how it will interact with users.

In the building phase, it's crucial to keep in mind that a conversation with a VUI is a two-way street. The VUI isn't just delivering information; it's also listening and responding to the user. Therefore, we need to design our VUI to understand and respond to a variety of user commands. Consider all the different ways a user might phrase a command or question and design your VUI to respond appropriately to these variations.

Next, we need to consider the personality of our VUI. Yes, you heard that right, personality! While it may seem strange to think of a machine as having a personality, in the world of VUIs, it can make a significant difference. A VUI's personality is conveyed through its tone of voice, its manner of speaking, and even the words it uses. It should reflect the brand and resonate with the users.

Once we've planned out our conversation and defined our VUI's personality, it's time to build. There are several great platforms out there for building VUIs, such as Amazon Alexa Skills Kit, Google Actions, and Microsoft's Bot Framework. These platforms provide tools that help with everything from defining the conversation flow to deploying your VUI.

Don't forget, building a VUI is an iterative process. It involves a cycle of building, testing, refining, and then testing again. When testing, look out for points of confusion or frustration for the user. Pay attention to where they might get stuck or misunderstand the VUI. Use these insights to refine and improve your design.

Once the VUI is built and refined, it's ready for deployment. But remember, deployment isn't the end of the process. Just like with any product, post-launch feedback is invaluable. Continue to gather feedback and make improvements after the VUI is live.

Building a VUI may seem daunting, but remember, every step of the journey offers a new learning opportunity. The world of VUIs is rapidly evolving, and as creators, we have the privilege of shaping its future. By creating VUIs that offer intuitive, engaging, and meaningful interactions, we can contribute to a world where technology feels less like an impersonal machine and more like a helpful companion.

5 /
accessibility in chat and voice ux

designing for inclusivity

IN OUR EXPLORATION of UX design, we've covered an array of topics, each crucial in its own right. Today, we delve into a particularly vital area: designing for inclusivity. It's about making sure our designs can be used, understood, and appreciated by all people, regardless of their abilities, age, gender, culture, language, or any other factors. Let's learn how to create inclusive designs that truly embrace all users.

Inclusive design is, at its core, a human-centric approach. It acknowledges the full range of human diversity with respect to ability, language, culture, gender, age, and other forms of human difference. The ultimate goal is to ensure that everyone can fully and equally participate in societal and economic life.

When designing for inclusivity, one of the key considerations is accessibility. This refers to designing products, devices, services, or environments for people who experience disabilities. When thinking about accessibility, it's crucial to consider the full range of abilities, including vision, hearing, cognition, and mobility.

For instance, if we're designing a VUI, we might include features like adjustable speech rates for those with hearing impairments or learning disabilities. Or, if we're designing a chat interface, we might ensure it's compatible with screen readers for visually impaired users. Considering these factors from the outset of your design process can make a significant difference in accessibility.

Cultural sensitivity is another essential component of inclusive design. This is about recognizing and respecting cultural differences and avoiding stereotypes or biased assumptions. For example, if you're designing a VUI, consider the cultural implications of your chosen voice or dialect. You'll want to ensure that your design communicates effectively and respectfully with users from diverse cultural backgrounds.

Let's also talk about age inclusivity. Technology is for everyone, not just the young. Therefore, it's essential to design our interfaces to be user-friendly for all age groups. This may mean increasing text size or simplifying navigation for older users. Or, for younger users, it might involve using simpler language and providing clear instructions.

Gender neutrality is yet another aspect of inclusive design. It's about ensuring your design doesn't favor any particular gender or make assumptions based on gender. For instance, if you're designing a chatbot, consider using a neutral name and avatar and avoiding gender-specific language.

Finally, designing for inclusivity also means being open to feedback and ready to make changes. This is where user testing comes in. By testing your design with a diverse group of users, you can uncover any inclusivity issues and work to resolve them. This testing should be ongoing, as inclusivity is a dynamic goal that requires continuous effort and improvement.

Inclusive design isn't just a checklist or an afterthought—it's a mindset. It should be at the heart of everything we do as UX designers. It's about designing not for some of us but for all of us, recognizing and celebrating the diversity of the human experience.

As we wrap up this section, let's hold on to the essence of inclusive design—a commitment to create technology that is accessible, respectful, and beneficial to all. As we move forward, may we always strive to design with empathy, respect, and a genuine under-standing of the beautiful diversity of our users. In the next section, we'll continue our journey, building on these principles to explore further aspects of user experience design. Join me, and let's learn together.

understanding accessibility standards

In the world of UX design, accessibility is a cornerstone principle. It means that products, services, and environments should be usable by all people, to the greatest extent possible, without modification. Accessibility standards provide the roadmap to ensure we're meeting this goal, offering guidelines that cover a variety of user needs and abilities.

One of the most prominent sets of guidelines is the Web Content Accessibility Guidelines (WCAG), developed by the World Wide Web Consortium (W3C). These are globally recognized standards aimed at making web content more accessible for people with disabilities, including blindness and low vision, deafness and hearing loss, limited movement, speech disabilities, and more.

WCAG guidelines are organized around four key principles, which are easy to remember with the acronym POUR: Perceivable, Operable, Understandable, and Robust.

1. Perceivable: This principle states that users must be able to perceive the information being presented. It

can't be invisible to all of their senses. For instance, offering text alternatives for non-text content, captions for audio or video, and ensuring content can be presented in different ways without losing meaning, such as simplifying layout.

2. Operable: This means that users must be able to operate the interface. All functionality should be available from a keyboard, and users should have enough time to read and use content. For instance, if a person has a motor disability and can't use a mouse, they should be able to navigate using a keyboard or voice commands.

3. Understandable: Information and operation of the user interface must be understandable. For example, content should be readable and understandable, and web pages should appear and operate in predictable ways. The interface should not behave in a way that confuses or disorients users.

4. Robust: Content must be robust enough to be interpreted reliably by a wide variety of user agents, including assistive technologies. In other words, the design should play well with current and future user tools.

Another important set of standards is the Americans with Disabilities Act (ADA), which requires businesses to make accommodations for people with disabilities in all their web content.

Similarly, section 508 of the Rehabilitation Act mandates federal agencies to make their electronic and information technology (EIT) accessible to people with disabilities. This covers web, software, and hardware accessibility, among other things.

Understanding these accessibility standards is key to developing empathetic and effective designs. However, it's important to remember that these are just guidelines, not the be-all and end-all. At the end of the day, the goal is to create products that can be used by as many people as possible, and there's always room to innovate within and beyond these standards.

tools and techniques for accessibility

Remember, a good designer is like a master craftsman. Just as a carpenter wouldn't dream of building a chair without a saw and hammer, you shouldn't dream of designing an accessible interface without the right tools and techniques.

There is a broad array of tools and techniques that designers can use to ensure their creations are accessible. These range from digital tools and software platforms, to human-centered research methods, to design and coding techniques. Let's unpack some of them.

Starting with digital tools, many software platforms and web-based applications exist to help designers audit their creations for accessibility. These include screen readers like NVDA or JAWS, which can simulate the experience of visually impaired users. They read aloud text and describe images, helping you understand how your design sounds to someone who can't see it.

Next, you've got color contrast checkers, like the WebAIM Color Contrast Checker. These tools analyze your color choices to ensure there's enough contrast for users who might be color blind or have low vision. Remember, it's not just about making things pretty; it's about making things clear and usable!

Tools like the WAVE Evaluation Tool can give your design a full accessibility workout, checking against a range of criteria and providing a report on any issues found. It's like a personal trainer for your design, spotting you as you lift heavy accessibility standards.

However, not all tools are digital. Some of the best techniques for ensuring accessibility involve good old-fashioned user research. User testing, especially with users who have disabilities, can provide invaluable insights into the accessibility of your designs. These testing sessions can be conducted in person or remotely, using a variety of methods from think-aloud protocols to observing users as they interact with your design.

Moreover, inclusive design workshops and

empathy mapping exercises can be powerful tech-niques for understanding the needs and desires of users with diverse abilities. These methods encourage designers to put themselves in the shoes of their users, cultivating a deep, empathetic understanding that guides their design decisions.

Then, there are design and coding techniques that can help ensure accessibility. For instance, when designing, you can use larger clickable targets to accommodate users with motor disabilities. When coding, you can use semantic HTML to help screen readers better understand your content.

Remember ARIA (Accessible Rich Internet Applications)? These are a set of attributes that define ways to make web content and web applications more accessible. They can be used to improve the accessi-bility and interoperability of web content and applications, especially when developing complex user interfaces or when using new or innovative web tech-nologies.

And let's not forget about accessible typography. By choosing fonts that are easier to read and by control-ling font size, line height, and letter spacing, you can make your text more accessible to a wide range of readers. The use of headers, bullets, and white space also contribute to readability.

We've covered a lot, but it's worth noting that this is

not an exhaustive list. Accessibility, like all aspects of UX, is a dynamic field, and new tools and techniques are being developed all the time. It's part of our job to stay updated, to keep learning, and to continually strive for better, more inclusive design.

6 /
best practices for
chat and voice ux

user-centred design approach

BY NOW, we have touched upon many aspects of UX design, from understanding our audience to the importance of accessibility. The next logical step is to go a bit deeper into the heart of our process – a user-centred design approach.

User-centred design (UCD) is a methodology that places users at the core of design decisions. In essence, it's about being a user advocate – prioritizing their needs, wants, and limitations over all other considerations. The central premise is this: by understanding your users' context and perspectives, you can create products that are more effective, efficient, and enjoyable.

The UCD approach is based on a few fundamental

principles. One of the most important of these is empathy. As UX professionals, it's our job to understand the users' thoughts, feelings, and frustrations. We have to "walk a mile in their shoes," so to speak. This understanding goes beyond mere demographics and involves developing a deep, empathetic understanding of the people for whom we are designing.

Another key aspect of UCD is iterative design. This means we don't design everything at once, but rather, we design, test, gather feedback, and repeat. By doing this, we continually refine and improve our designs based on real user feedback. It's a dynamic process – much like a conversation that evolves over time.

Now, you might be wondering: "How do we actually put these principles into practice?" Well, there are several techniques we can employ to implement a UCD approach. Let's explore some of them.

The first stage in the UCD process is understanding the user. There are many ways to do this, but some common methods include user interviews, observations, and surveys. These techniques allow us to gather qualitative and quantitative data about our users – their needs, their behaviors, their pain points. By interpreting this data, we can develop user personas and user stories, which help guide our design decisions.

Once we have a firm understanding of our users, the

next step is ideation – generating a range of possible design solutions. This stage often involves techniques like brainstorming, sketching, or creating low-fidelity wireframes. The goal here is to explore as many different design options as possible, and to start shaping our ideas based on the user data we have gathered.

Next comes prototyping. This involves creating more detailed, interactive representations of our designs. These prototypes might still be quite rough, but they should be functional enough to give users a realistic sense of how the final product will work.

Following prototyping, we move into user testing. This involves presenting our prototypes to users and observing how they interact with them. The feedback we gather during user testing is invaluable. It helps us understand what's working, what's not, and what we could do better.

Finally, we refine our designs based on the feedback received, and then we repeat the process. Yes, you heard it right! We go back to prototyping, testing, and refining until we are confident that we have a product that meets our users' needs.

By adopting a UCD approach, we ensure that we're creating products that are not only functional and usable, but also enjoyable and meaningful. It's like cooking a meal for someone: you need to understand their tastes and dietary needs to create a meal they'll love.

This user-centred design journey is a beautiful one. It's an ongoing conversation between the designer and the user, a dance of insights, iterations, and improvements. And it's a journey that rewards us with the ultimate prize: products that truly serve our users and add value to their lives.

utilizing feedback effectively

As UX practitioners, one of the most critical parts of our work is handling feedback. The design process is never a one-way street; it's a continual loop of creating, sharing, receiving feedback, and iterating. But how can we utilize that feedback effectively to improve our work? That's the question we'll be exploring in this section.

First and foremost, let's establish that feedback is a gift. Yes, you heard it right! Even if it sometimes feels uncomfortable, feedback is a treasure trove of insights that can make our designs better, more user-friendly, and more impactful. However, this is only true if we know how to accept, analyze, and apply it correctly.

The first step in utilizing feedback effectively is to create a safe space for it. This means establishing an environment where feedback is expected, encouraged, and respected. A healthy feedback culture begins with open-mindedness. We have to be ready to listen, to understand, and to accept that our designs can always be improved.

One way to foster this culture is by actively seeking feedback. Don't wait for it to come to you; request it. Reach out to colleagues, superiors, or even users. You'll be surprised at the insights you can glean from different perspectives.

Next, when receiving feedback, it's important to listen actively. This means not just hearing the words, but truly trying to understand the underlying message. Ask clarifying questions if needed. Don't be defensive; instead, try to view the feedback from the giver's perspective.

However, it's also crucial to remember that not all feedback should be acted upon. As UX practitioners, we should be adept at filtering and categorizing feedback. Some feedback will be insightful and directly applicable. Some might be valuable but need a little reinterpretation. Other feedback might not be relevant at all.

Remember, as a designer, you have a deep understanding of your project's goals and constraints. You are uniquely positioned to evaluate the feasibility and value of the feedback you receive. Use this understanding to decide which feedback to act upon.

Once you have a collection of valuable feedback, it's time to start iterating. Use the insights you've gathered to refine your designs. Try to address the issues raised, but don't forget about the broader context of your work. Every design decision you make will have ripple effects, so always consider the big picture.

After iterating on your designs, it's back to feedback gathering again. Remember, the design process is iterative. Every round of feedback and revision brings you closer to a design solution that truly meets your users' needs and wants.

It's also essential to keep in mind that feedback should not only be used to fix problems but also to recognize successes. Celebrating the aspects of your work that others see as effective or innovative can be incredibly motivating. It highlights what to carry forward into future projects.

Lastly, remember to be gracious. Always thank your feedback givers. They've taken the time to help you improve your work, and that deserves appreciation. Plus, fostering positive relationships will make people more likely to provide you with valuable feedback in the future.

continuous improvement and testing

Continuous improvement, as the name suggests, is an ongoing effort to improve products, services, or processes. It's not about making large, sweeping changes all at once; instead, it's about making small, incremental changes consistently over time. In UX, continuous improvement focuses on enhancing the user experience by constantly evolving and refining the product or service based on user feedback and testing.

This process starts with a solid understanding of your users, their needs, and their pain points. You've already done the groundwork in identifying your audience, creating personas, and understanding their journey. This information serves as your baseline for improvement.

Next, we gather data and feedback. You have many tools at your disposal, from user surveys and interviews to analytics and heatmaps. The key is to gather both quantitative and qualitative data. Quantitative data, like click-through rates or time spent on a page, gives you an overview of user behavior. Qualitative data, such as user interviews or open-ended survey responses, helps you understand the 'why' behind these behaviors.

Once you've gathered this data, it's time to analyze it. Look for trends, anomalies, or anything that sticks out. This is where your detective skills come into play. Remember to keep an open mind and avoid jumping to conclusions. The goal is to form hypotheses based on your findings, not to confirm pre-existing beliefs.

After analyzing your data and forming hypotheses, you plan and implement changes based on your insights. Maybe you've noticed users struggling with a particular feature, or perhaps they're not engaging with a part of your website as much as you'd like. Whatever the issue, you now have the insight to make informed changes to address it.

Now, you might be thinking that once the changes are made, the job is done. But in the world of UX, we're just getting started! This is where testing comes into play.

Testing is the backbone of continuous improvement. It allows us to validate our hypotheses and measure the effectiveness of our changes. There are numerous ways to conduct testing in UX. Usability testing, A/B testing, first-click testing, the list goes on. The method you choose will depend on what you're trying to learn.

Usability testing, for example, is great for understanding how users interact with your product and identifying any issues they may encounter. A/B testing, on the other hand, is excellent for comparing two different versions of a design element to see which performs better.

After testing, it's time to review the results and gather insights. Did the changes have the desired effect? Were there unexpected outcomes? These findings will inform your next steps and your ongoing improvement cycle.

And then, with fresh insights in hand, you start the process all over again. This is the heart of continuous improvement – the cycle of gathering data, making changes, testing, and learning.

In the world of UX, this is not a one-time process but rather a constant, ongoing cycle. It's important to remember that the goal is not perfection, but betterment. We are not trying to create a perfect product or service (though that would be nice!), but rather one that continuously evolves to meet our users' changing needs and expectations.

future-proofing your designs

Let's dive into another exciting topic today: future-proofing your designs. The digital landscape is perpetually evolving, and as creators in this space, it's our responsibility to create products that can withstand the test of time. We don't have a crystal ball to predict the future, but there are strategies we can employ to ensure our designs stay relevant and functional, regardless of what the future brings.

Now, when we talk about future-proofing, it doesn't mean creating a design that will never need updates or improvements. That's an impossible task. Technologies and user behaviors are continually changing, and our designs must adapt accordingly. Instead, future-proofing is about thinking ahead, anticipating changes, and building flexibility into your designs to make those inevitable updates more manageable.

Future-proofing starts with the adoption of a flexible and modular design system. A design system, if you're not familiar with the term, is a collection of reusable components guided by clear standards that can be assembled together to build any number of applications. It's like a box of LEGO bricks. Each brick can be used in countless ways to create different structures. Similarly, a well-constructed design system allows you to quickly adapt to changing needs and technologies.

Next, ensure your designs are responsive and adaptable across a range of devices and platforms. With the multitude of devices available today and the certainty of more to come, a design that only looks good on one type of device is already outdated. Implement responsive design principles to ensure your design is flexible and adapts to different screen sizes and orientations.

Interoperability is another key element of future-proof design. Your product should play well with others. This means making sure it can integrate smoothly with other systems, platforms, and technologies that your users might adopt in the future. This might involve adopting widely used standards and protocols, providing a robust API, or simply ensuring your code is clean and well-documented for future developers.

Embrace emerging technologies, but don't be led by them. It's easy to get caught up in the latest tech trends, but it's essential to remember that new technology should serve the design, not the other way around. The goal is to enhance the user experience, so if a new technology doesn't contribute to that, it may not be worth adopting.

Accessibility and inclusivity must also be a core part of your design strategy. As our understanding of the diverse range of users' needs continues to evolve, making your designs accessible is not just about future-proofing—it's about good design. Build with accessibility in mind from the outset, and your designs will be better positioned to accommodate future changes in accessibility standards and guidelines.

Lastly, make data your ally. Monitor how users

interact with your designs, gather feedback, and continually test and iterate. This will not only improve your current designs but also provide valuable insights that can inform your future design decisions.

Future-proofing is a bit like navigating a ship. You might not be able to control the wind or the waves, but with a well-built ship and a skilled crew, you can navigate successfully through whatever comes your way. Your designs, too, can be built to weather the storms of change, evolving technologies, and shifting user expectations.

7 /
ethical
considerations in ux
design

data privacy and security

DATA PRIVACY and security are more than mere buzzwords in our modern age—they're essential elements in building trust and providing quality user experiences. As we collect, store, and analyze user data to enhance our designs, it's our responsibility to ensure that data is handled with utmost respect and integrity.

Firstly, let's establish a key principle: data minimization. As designers, we should only collect the necessary data we need to fulfill a specific purpose. This means being thoughtful and selective about what information we collect from users and being transparent about why we need it. In addition, we should only retain the data for as long as needed. This reduces the potential harm in the event of a data breach and respects the privacy of our users.

Now, let's talk about encryption. Encrypting data is a fundamental aspect of data security. By converting data into code, we prevent unauthorized access. This should be done for data at rest (stored data) and data in transit (data being transferred). SSL and TLS protocols are common methods of ensuring data in transit remains secure.

Implementing strong access controls is another important strategy. Not everyone in your organization needs access to all data. Implementing role-based access control (RBAC) is one way to ensure that only those who need to access certain data can do so. Moreover, multifactor authentication provides an additional layer of security.

Now, on to a topic that's particularly pertinent - consent. As part of respecting user privacy, always seek user consent before collecting and processing their data. Be clear and upfront about what data you're collecting, why you're collecting it, and how you plan to use it. This builds trust with users and reinforces the idea that they are in control of their own data.

One cannot stress enough the importance of having a robust and comprehensive privacy policy in place. This document should clearly outline all the measures you're taking to protect user data. Additionally, it should detail the rights of the user in relation to their data, including the right to access, correct, or delete their data.

Always remember, though, that privacy and security measures are not a one-and-done affair. Regular audits and updates are necessary to ensure these measures remain effective and up-to-date with current regulations and technologies.

Bear in mind that while some of these concepts may seem more relevant to developers or security professionals, they're crucial for anyone involved in the creation of a digital product. As designers, understanding and advocating for data privacy and security can greatly influence the decisions we make and the experiences we create.

To wrap things up, data privacy and security aren't just about following laws and regulations—they're about treating users with respect and maintaining their trust. While it's easy to get caught up in the excitement of creating visually stunning and functionally impressive designs, we should never forget the human element in the digital equation.

user consent and transparency

User consent and transparency are fundamental elements in maintaining this trust. In essence, it's about openly communicating with users, explaining what data you're collecting, why you're collecting it, how it will be used, and then obtaining their explicit consent for these actions.

When thinking about user consent, the first thing to note is that it needs to be freely given, informed, and explicit. This means that the user must be provided with a real choice and control. Pre-ticked boxes or any element of force or compulsion should be avoided. It's also important that the consent is specific and granular, meaning that it covers the specific processing operations and purposes.

A crucial part of obtaining informed consent is providing clear, concise, and easy-to-understand information. It's no secret that many of us have clicked 'agree' on a cookie banner or terms and conditions without reading the full text. To combat this, strive to present the necessary information in a user-friendly way. This can include layering information, using just-in-time notices, and visual cues.

Now, let's touch on the concept of transparency. Transparency in a digital context means providing clear, timely, and comprehensive information about how and why data is being processed. Essentially, it's about being open and honest with users.

One way to foster transparency is by providing clear and accessible privacy notices. However, transparency goes beyond the privacy policy. It also covers how you communicate changes to data practices, how you handle data breaches, and how you respond to user queries and complaints.

Moreover, transparency extends to the algorithms and AI systems we use. Algorithmic transparency involves being open about how decisions are made by algorithms, especially those that can significantly impact users. As we create more complex systems, it's crucial that we consider how to make these understandable to users.

A final consideration is the right to withdraw consent. Remember, consent should not be a one-time event. Users have the right to change their mind and withdraw their consent at any time, and it should be as easy to withdraw consent as it is to give it. Providing easy-to-use and accessible mechanisms for users to manage their consent is an essential part of respectful design.

Bringing this all together, user consent and transparency aren't just legal requirements or boxes to be ticked off a checklist. They're about fostering trust and respect with users. They're about acknowledging the value and importance of user data, and recognizing the inherent human rights to privacy and control over one's information.

bias in design

The previous section led us through the essentials of user consent and transparency, and now we're going to dig a little deeper into ethical design. Specifically, we'll look at how bias can unintentionally creep into our design process and what we can do to mitigate its effects.

Firstly, let's define bias. Bias, in the context of design, refers to tendencies or preconceptions that influence our decision-making process. These biases can stem from our backgrounds, experiences, and personal preferences. While it's impossible to completely eliminate bias, recognizing and managing it can help us create more inclusive and equitable designs.

Biases can take many forms. They can be conscious or unconscious, and they can be related to any number of characteristics, such as age, gender, race, socioeconomic status, or physical ability. Regardless of the form they take, biases can negatively impact the inclusivity and effectiveness of our designs if not addressed.

So, how can bias sneak into design? Well, bias can emerge at any stage of the design process, from user research to ideation, prototyping, and testing. For example, if we only conduct user research with a narrow group of users, our results might not represent the needs of all potential users. This can lead to designs that inadvertently exclude certain groups.

Now, onto the more crucial question: how do we address bias in design? There are a few strategies that can help.

Firstly, we need to broaden our understanding and empathy. Empathy is a key skill in design, as it allows us to understand and design for the needs of diverse users. We can develop our empathy through methods like user interviews, empathy maps, and personas. However, it's important to ensure these tools represent a diverse range of users and are not based solely on our own experiences or assumptions.

Secondly, we need to diversify our teams. Diverse teams bring a wider range of perspectives and experiences to the table, helping to challenge and reduce bias. Diversity isn't just about ethnicity or gender; it's also about having a range of ages, abilities, backgrounds, and experiences represented in your team.

Thirdly, we should aim for inclusivity in user research and testing. By including a diverse range of users in your research and testing phases, you can identify and address issues that may not be visible from your own perspective. Techniques like inclusive persona development and co-designing with users can be particularly helpful here.

Lastly, and most importantly, we must always be

open to feedback and willing to iterate our designs. Even with the best intentions and most rigorous processes, some bias may still creep into our designs. However, by welcoming feedback and being willing to adjust our designs based on this feedback, we can continually work towards more inclusive and equitable solutions.

In sum, bias is an inherent part of being human. But that doesn't mean we're powerless to address it in our work. By recognizing and actively working to mitigate bias in our designs, we can create more inclusive, accessible, and effective experiences for all users.

8 /
tools for designing chat and voice ux

overview of industry-standard tools

IT'S time to get our hands metaphorically dirty with some practical stuff. This section will explore the tools of the trade, giving you a guided tour of the industry-standard tools that bring our designs to life.

First off, it's crucial to remember that no single tool can be the magic solution to all design needs. Each project and team will have unique requirements and preferences, so the key is to be adaptable and versatile. Let's now delve into some of the most commonly used tools in various areas of design.

Let's start with prototyping and wireframing tools. These tools allow designers to create a skeleton of the final design, mapping out the layout and functionality without getting into the nitty-gritty of visual design.

Sketch is a popular choice for its simplicity and power, while Axure RP is prized for its advanced interactive features. Adobe XD and Figma offer collaborative capabilities that are incredibly useful for teams.

Next, let's look at graphic design tools. Adobe's suite of tools, including Illustrator, Photoshop, and InDesign, are the industry standards here. They provide a wide range of capabilities from photo editing and vector graphics to layout design. Meanwhile, tools like Canva offer simplified and intuitive design capabilities that can be perfect for smaller projects or for those just starting in design.

For user interface design, tools like Figma and Sketch dominate. They allow designers to create both low-fidelity and high-fidelity designs with ease, and they have powerful plugin ecosystems that extend their capabilities. Adobe XD is another strong contender, particularly for teams already embedded in the Adobe ecosystem.

User testing and feedback tools are also vital in the design process. UsabilityHub allows for quick and straightforward user testing, while UserTesting provides more in-depth feedback and insights. Hotjar offers heatmaps and user session recordings to help understand user behavior, while Maze allows for inter-active prototype testing.

For collaboration and handoff, look to tools like

Zeplin and InVision. These platforms allow designers to share their designs with developers and stakeholders, ensuring everyone is on the same page and making the handoff process smoother. They automatically generate specs and resources that developers need, saving time and reducing potential misunderstandings.

On the project management side, tools like Trello, Asana, or Jira are popular. They help teams keep track of tasks, manage workflows, and ensure everyone stays in sync. These tools are not design-specific, but their role in a smoothly running design project cannot be overstated.

Remember, these tools are just that - tools. They are there to assist you, not dictate your process. The right tools for you will depend on various factors like your team's size, the specifics of the project, the budget, and your personal preferences. Don't be afraid to try out different tools and find the ones that fit your workflow best.

In the world of design, the only constant is change. New tools are constantly emerging, each with their own strengths and weaknesses. Stay curious and adaptable, and don't be afraid to try new things. After all, every tool you learn and skill you develop adds to your design toolbox, making you a more versatile and effective designer.

pros and cons of popular tools

Having explored the landscape of industry-standard design tools in the previous section, we are now ready to dive a bit deeper. In this section, we'll consider the pros and cons of some of these popular tools, shedding light on their strengths, limitations, and ideal use-cases. This knowledge will empower you to choose the right tool for the right task, a key skill for any seasoned professional.

Let's start with Sketch, one of the most beloved tools in the UI/UX design community. Sketch's pros lie in its simplicity, efficiency, and powerful features for interface design. It offers a user-friendly interface, excellent rendering, and a broad range of plugins. However, it's only available for Mac, which can be a significant con if your team uses different operating systems. Furthermore, it lacks certain prototyping and collaboration capabilities compared to other tools.

Figma, another favorite, shines in its browser-based interface that enables real-time collaboration, much like Google Docs for design. Its prototyping features are top-notch, and it's available on multiple platforms. The con of Figma could be its performance with larger files; it can become slower, impacting productivity.

Adobe XD, part of Adobe's creative suite, boasts seamless integration with other Adobe products. This is a major pro if you're already using Adobe's ecosystem. XD is also straightforward to use, offers solid prototyping and collaboration features, and works across platforms. The con, however, is its limited extensibility compared to Sketch and Figma, as it doesn't support as many plugins.

When it comes to wireframing, Axure RP stands out with its rich features for creating highly interactive and dynamic prototypes. However, its learning curve is steeper than other tools, making it less suitable for beginners. Also, it can feel a bit clunky and old-fashioned compared to sleeker, newer tools.

UsabilityHub is a brilliant tool for quick and basic user testing, ideal for getting feedback fast. Its main con is that it's not as comprehensive as other testing tools. On the other hand, UserTesting provides deeper insights but can be overkill (and expensive) for smaller or simpler projects.

In the realm of project management tools, Trello is lauded for its simplicity and flexibility. It uses a board-based system that's intuitive and easy to use. On the downside, for complex projects with many tasks and dependencies, Trello can quickly become overwhelming. In contrast, Asana and Jira offer more structure and powerful features to handle complex projects, but they have a steeper learning curve and can be overkill for smaller projects or teams.

Zeplin and InVision are fantastic for collaboration and handoff. Zeplin excels at generating accurate specs, assets, and code snippets, making developers' lives easier. However, it does not support actual design creation. InVision, on the other hand, has a range of design and prototyping tools, but its handoff features are not as automated as Zeplin's.

And finally, when it comes to graphic design, Adobe's Photoshop and Illustrator remain the gold standard due to their power and flexibility. But their complexity and cost can be daunting for beginners or smaller teams. Canva provides a more accessible, though less powerful, alternative.

Whew! That was quite the run-through, but remember, this isn't a competition. Each tool has its place, and the best tool depends on the task at hand, the specifics of the project, and the makeup of the team. It's about using the right tool at the right time.

9 /
case studies in chat and voice ux

examination of successful designs

AFTER CHOOSING the perfect tools for your project, we now turn our attention to the study of successful designs. By examining and understanding what makes a design successful, we can better apply these principles to our own work. Let's dive in and see what we can glean from some of the best designs out there.

At the outset, let's appreciate that a design's success isn't measured by its aesthetic appeal alone. While visual attractiveness is certainly a component, it is the combination of usability, relevance, and emotional connection that truly sets successful designs apart.

. . .

Let's start with a case that you'll undoubtedly be familiar with - the intuitive design of the iPhone interface. When the first iPhone launched, it wasn't just the technology that made it revolutionary - it was the simplicity and usability of the design. The home screen with rounded app icons, the minimalistic color scheme, the intuitive gestures - all of these design choices were aimed at creating an interface that was not just pleasing to the eye, but also user-friendly and efficient. This focus on the user's experience is a hallmark of successful design.

Consider also the example of Airbnb's website. It's a testament to thoughtful information architecture and clarity. The search bar is the hero of the homepage, signaling the website's primary function. High-quality images generate a sense of wanderlust, while clear, concise text makes navigation a breeze. Moreover, Airbnb employs an inclusive design approach, offering a variety of filtering options that cater to diverse user needs, such as accessible accommodations for people with disabilities. This illustrates the power of an empathetic, user-centric approach in successful design.

. . .

Now, let's take a glance at the world of physical products with the example of the OXO Good Grips line of kitchen tools. This line was designed with a specific problem in mind - making kitchen tools that were easy to handle, especially for those with arthritis. The tools feature large, non-slip handles that are designed to be ergonomic and comfortable. This clearly exhibits how effective problem-solving can lead to success in design.

Reflecting on these successful designs, there are certain common themes to observe. These designs are user-centric, they solve a problem effectively, and they establish an emotional connection with the user. They pay attention not just to the "what" and the "how", but also to the "why". They demonstrate a keen under-standing of the users' context, needs, and desires.

As a design professional, it's valuable to regularly examine and learn from successful designs like these. Not only should we appreciate these designs, but also critically analyze them. Ask yourself: What problem does this design solve? How does it improve the user's experience? What emotional response does it elicit? How does it cater to diverse user needs? How does it balance aesthetics with functionality?

. . .

By analyzing successful designs in this way, you can derive insights that inform and inspire your own work. You can understand the principles and strategies that underpin effective design, and apply these learnings to create designs that are equally successful and impactful.

lessons from failed designs

Design failures can take many forms, from poorly planned websites and confusing user interfaces to product designs that completely miss the mark. Let's examine some notorious examples to see what lessons we can glean.

Starting in the digital realm, recall the redesign of Snapchat in 2018. Snapchat's goal was to separate social interactions from media content, seemingly a thoughtful decision for improving user experience. However, the end result was a confusing interface that blended stories from friends with those of celebrities, leading to a significant backlash from the user community. User engagement dropped drastically, causing the company to roll back many changes.

. . .

This instance highlights the importance of thoroughly understanding your user's needs and expectations before implementing significant design changes. Changes should enhance the user experience, not complicate it. Rigorous user testing before full roll-out is critical to ensure that the redesigned product meets user needs and avoids unnecessary complexity.

Moving to physical products, remember the case of the Juicero, a high-tech juicer that was marketed as a revolutionary device. However, it was soon discovered that the juice packs could be squeezed just as effectively by hand, rendering the expensive device unnecessary. This case underscores the importance of ensuring that a design is not just innovative but also practical and cost-effective. A design should solve a problem, not create a new one.

We also have the case of Google Glass. While undeniably innovative, Google Glass was criticized for its high price, lack of clear purpose, privacy concerns, and, importantly, its design. Wearing Google Glass made users stand out, and not in a way most people found desirable. This experience underlines the fact that while technology is a crucial element in design, it's not the only factor. Aesthetics and social acceptability are also vital aspects of a product's design, especially when it's something to be worn.

While it's never pleasant to focus on failures, each of these cases offers valuable design lessons. They stress the need for thorough user testing, understanding the needs and desires of the target audience, practicality, cost-effectiveness, and the critical balance between technology and design.

As design professionals, it's crucial to remember that failure is not the end, but an opportunity for learning and growth. When designs fail, they provide an opportunity to understand what went wrong and why. As we reflect on these design failures, we can extract valuable lessons that can guide us towards more successful design outcomes in our own work.

exploring innovative approaches

Innovation in design often emerges from combining existing ideas in new ways or challenging the status quo. To successfully innovate, we must think outside the box, break rules, and take risks. However, these risks should be calculated, informed by user needs, and validated through testing and iteration, as we have discussed in previous sections.

One of the most exciting frontiers in design today is the integration of artificial intelligence (AI). AI and machine learning can help automate and improve many aspects of design. AI tools can analyze large amounts of user data to gain deep insights about user behaviors and preferences, which can inform design decisions. These technologies can also aid in automated design generation, enabling rapid iteration and testing of design ideas.

A notable example of AI in design is the use of generative design in architecture and product design. Generative design uses algorithms to create a wide variety of design options based on specified parameters. This approach enables designers to explore a vast design space quickly, selecting the most promising ideas for further refinement.

. . .

Immersive technologies like augmented reality (AR) and virtual reality (VR) are also bringing innovation to the design field. These technologies provide new ways to visualize and interact with designs. AR and VR can be used for virtual prototyping, allowing designers and stakeholders to experience a design in a realistic way before it is built. This capability can speed up the design process, save costs, and enable more effective communication of design ideas.

Another innovative approach is the use of biodesign, integrating natural processes and biological materials into design. Biodesign can lead to products and systems that are sustainable, adaptive, and in harmony with the natural world. Examples include using mycelium (the root structure of mushrooms) for packaging or building materials, or integrating living plants into architectural structures.

Design for social innovation is another frontier, using design thinking to address societal challenges. This approach involves collaborating with communities, understanding their needs deeply, and co-creating solutions that can have a positive social impact.

· · ·

Finally, the trend towards personalization is pushing the boundaries of design. With the aid of data and technology, products can now be tailored to individual users' needs and preferences, providing a unique user experience.

10 /
future trends in
chat and voice ux

emerging technologies impacting ux

AS WE'RE ABOUT to find out, the world of technology is forever changing, and these changes are influencing user experience (UX) design in remarkable ways. Let's examine some of the emerging technologies that are reshaping the UX landscape.

First on our list is Artificial Intelligence (AI). It's impossible to overstate the impact of AI on UX. For instance, AI-powered chatbots are changing how businesses interact with customers online, providing round-the-clock service and instant responses. However, for a truly effective UX, the challenge lies in making these interactions feel as natural and human-like as possible. Machine learning algorithms help to improve these responses over time, leading to increasingly sophisticated conversations.

Virtual Reality (VR) and Augmented Reality (AR) are next up, dramatically changing our perception of space and place. VR offers completely immersive experiences, bringing users into new, fully digital environments. AR, on the other hand, overlays digital information onto the real world, enhancing the user's immediate surroundings. From a UX standpoint, these technologies open a new universe of possibilities for interacting with digital content.

Voice User Interfaces (VUI) are becoming more common, powered by AI-driven assistants like Amazon's Alexa, Apple's Siri, and Google Assistant. As we move towards a more hands-free digital world, creating a UX for VUIs requires a different approach than graphical interfaces. It's all about creating a seamless conversation with the user, understanding their commands, and providing clear, concise responses.

. . .

Blockchain is another transformative technology. While it's best known as the technology underpinning cryptocurrencies, its potential uses extend far beyond. Blockchain can create secure, transparent digital systems where all transactions are recorded and visible to all participants. The UX challenge here lies in making these complex systems accessible and understandable to the average user.

Internet of Things (IoT) is also revolutionizing UX. As everyday objects become "smart" and connected to the internet, they generate a vast amount of data that can be used to improve the UX. For instance, a smart fridge could suggest recipes based on what's inside, providing a more personalized and useful experience for the user. But, the critical issue here is the handling of this personal data, maintaining user privacy and security.

Finally, there's 5G - the latest generation of mobile internet connectivity. With its promise of faster speeds and more reliable connections, 5G will enable more complex and data-intensive applications to run smoothly on mobile devices. From a UX perspective, this means that designers can create more detailed, immersive, and interactive experiences without worrying about slow load times or connection issues.

While the potential of these technologies is enormous, it's essential to remember that they are tools to enhance the user's experience. It's easy to get caught up in the excitement of new technology and forget the fundamental goal of UX design: to create products that meet users' needs in a meaningful way.

predictions for chat and voice ux

Given the exciting developments we've seen in technology, we are poised to witness some remarkable transformations in this domain.

To kick things off, let's consider the realm of chat UX. One anticipated trend is the evolution of chatbots from rule-based systems to AI-powered ones. Currently, most chatbots function based on pre-set rules and programmed responses. However, with advancements in AI and machine learning, we can expect chatbots to evolve significantly, providing more natural, personalized, and human-like interactions. This evolution will greatly enhance user experience by creating a sense of interaction with a real human.

In addition to this, the line between live chat and chatbots is expected to blur. A more collaborative model is likely, where chatbots handle routine queries and live agents intervene for more complex issues. This will allow businesses to provide superior service by leveraging the efficiency of bots while maintaining the personal touch of human interaction.

Another emerging trend in chat UX is the integration of more multimedia content. We can expect future chat systems to handle images, videos, and other interactive content seamlessly. This will not only make chats more engaging but also allow users to express themselves more fully and accurately.

Now, let's shift our focus to the world of voice UX. With the growing popularity of voice assistants like Alexa, Siri, and Google Assistant, voice interactions are becoming an integral part of our digital lives. The use of voice interfaces is expected to grow significantly, driven by their convenience and the natural feel of speech as a mode of interaction.

One prediction in this space is the rise of multimodal interfaces. These interfaces combine voice with other input methods like touch or gesture, offering users more flexibility in how they interact with devices. For example, a user might ask their smart display for a recipe, then swipe through the steps while cooking.

Alongside, we can expect more sophisticated voice recognition technology. Future systems will likely be able to understand a broader range of accents, dialects, and speech patterns, making voice interfaces accessible to a wider audience. This also ties in with the notion of inclusivity in design, a topic we've discussed earlier.

A vital part of the evolution of voice UX will be the enhancement of contextual understanding. Voice assistants will get better at understanding the context of conversations, remembering past interactions, and anticipating user needs. The challenge here is to make these interactions feel helpful rather than intrusive, ensuring users feel in control of their digital conversations.

As a note of caution, as chat and voice interactions become more complex and AI-driven, issues related to data privacy, user consent, and transparency become even more critical. We need to design systems that not only deliver superior UX but also respect user privacy and uphold ethical standards.

Peering into the future of chat and voice UX is indeed thrilling. The advancements we've discussed offer opportunities to create more engaging, intuitive, and human-like interactions. However, they also present challenges that we, as UX professionals, must thoughtfully navigate.

preparing for future trends

As we chart our course into the future of chat and voice UX, let's discuss the ways we can prepare ourselves to ride the wave of these upcoming trends. Just as a captain prepares their ship for a voyage, we need to equip ourselves with the right tools and mindset to navigate these promising yet unpredictable seas.

First and foremost, we should be open and adaptable to change. Technological landscapes, especially those as dynamic as chat and voice UX, are continuously evolving. Staying updated with these changes is not a luxury but a necessity for any UX professional. Follow industry news, attend webinars, engage in online communities, and don't hesitate to enroll in new courses when they become available. Education, after all, is an ongoing process.

Next, cultivate a deep understanding of AI and machine learning, as they are at the heart of many future trends in UX. It's not just about knowing the buzzwords; it's about understanding how these technologies work, their potential applications, and their implications for design. This doesn't mean you need to become a data scientist overnight, but having a solid grasp of AI and machine learning principles will make you a more informed and effective UX designer.

. . .

Thirdly, invest in learning about new tools and technologies. As we discussed in the previous sections, there's an array of tools available for UX design, each with its unique strengths and weaknesses. Stay informed about new software and platforms as they come to market. Make it a habit to test drive new tools as they appear. This hands-on approach can provide you invaluable insights and keep your skills sharp and relevant.

In the same vein, keep an eye on the rise of new interaction paradigms like gesture or gaze-based inter-actions. As voice and chat interfaces continue to evolve, they may start to incorporate or interface with these newer methods of interaction. Understanding these technologies now can put you a step ahead when they become more prevalent.

Another critical part of preparing for the future is building and maintaining a robust understanding of data privacy and security principles. As UX designers, we have a responsibility to create designs that not only offer a superior user experience but also protect user data. This topic will only become more relevant as voice and chat UX become more sophisticated and data-driven.

Additionally, practice inclusivity in design. As we've discussed, good UX is usable by as wide a range of people as possible. As new technologies emerge, it's our responsibility to ensure they are accessible and inclusive. Incorporate accessibility and inclusivity practices into your design process, and always consider a broad spectrum of users in your designs.

Furthermore, stay attuned to changes in user expectations. As users become more accustomed to advanced chat and voice interfaces, their expectations will evolve. Regular user research is crucial to understand these changing needs and preferences. Keep the lines of communication with users open, actively seek their feedback, and make adjustments based on their input.

Lastly, foster a culture of experimentation and iteration. Embrace the opportunity to experiment with new designs, measure their performance, and iterate on them based on your findings. Remember, every "failed" experiment is a chance to learn and improve.

Looking ahead, it's evident that the future of chat and voice UX is ripe with possibilities. Preparing for these future trends involves equipping ourselves with the necessary knowledge, skills, and mindset. It means being open to change, staying informed, embracing new technologies, and always putting the user at the center of our designs.

11 /
building your career
in chat and voice ux

essential skills for ux designers

AS WE REACH the end of our exploration into the fascinating world of chat and voice UX, let's reflect on the essential skills every UX designer should possess. These are the traits and skills that will help you not only navigate the waters of the present but also stay afloat as the tides of the future roll in.

First and foremost, UX designers need a solid understanding of user-centered design principles. As we've discussed throughout this guide, putting the user at the heart of your design process is crucial. This involves developing a deep understanding of your users' needs, desires, behaviors, and pain points, and using this understanding to inform your design decisions.

Next, let's talk about empathy. This skill goes hand-in-hand with user-centered design. Empathy allows us to truly understand and resonate with users' feelings and needs. It helps us design experiences that not only solve users' problems but also delight and engage them. If you can put yourself in the shoes of your users, you're well on your way to creating compelling user experiences.

Technical skills are another must-have in the UX designer's toolkit. This includes proficiency in design and prototyping tools, understanding of coding basics, and familiarity with UX testing methods. Keep in mind, though, that the tools you use will likely evolve as technology progresses, so staying up-to-date and adaptable is key.

Next up is knowledge of AI and machine learning, as they are becoming increasingly important in the realm of chat and voice UX. Having a grasp on how these technologies work and their implications for design will empower you to create more intelligent, user-friendly interfaces.

Of course, let's not forget about communication skills. As a UX designer, you'll often find yourself collaborating with various stakeholders, including developers, product managers, marketers, and of course, users. Being able to clearly and effectively communicate your ideas and designs is vital.

Alongside communication skills, teamwork and collaboration skills are equally important. The process of creating a great user experience is often a team effort. Knowing how to collaborate effectively, navigate team dynamics, give and receive feedback, and compromise when needed, is crucial.

Research skills are another essential element for UX designers. This encompasses conducting user research, performing usability testing, and analyzing user data. These research activities will provide valuable insights that can drive your design decisions.

Next, UX designers should have a keen eye for detail. The difference between a good user experience and a great one often lies in the small details. Attention to detail ensures that no aspect of the user experience is overlooked.

Understanding of accessibility standards and inclusive design practices is another essential skill. As designers, we have a responsibility to ensure our designs can be used and enjoyed by as wide a range of people as possible. This requires understanding and applying accessibility standards and principles in our designs.

Finally, problem-solving skills round out our list of essential skills for UX designers. At its core, UX design is about solving problems. It's about finding innovative solutions to users' challenges, and continuously iterating on these solutions to make them better.

Armed with these skills, you're prepared to take on the exciting challenges and opportunities in the world of chat and voice UX. Remember, though, that becoming a successful UX designer isn't a destination —it's a journey. Continuous learning and improvement are key. Stay curious, stay passionate, and don't be afraid to take risks.

tips for portfolio building

It's your chance to showcase your skills, projects, and most importantly, your unique approach to problem-solving and design thinking. So, let's dive into some tips on building a portfolio that truly represents you as a UX designer.

The first rule of thumb in portfolio creation is, quite simply, quality over quantity. This isn't the time or place to showcase every project you've ever worked on. Instead, cherry-pick your most impressive or innovative works, those that best demonstrate your skills, creativity, and adaptability. You want your portfolio to be a reflection of your best self.

Next, you want to consider your audience. Remember, your portfolio will likely be viewed by various stakeholders, including hiring managers, recruiters, and fellow designers. Make sure it communicates clearly to all of them. Tailor the information and level of detail to your audience's needs and expectations.

Moving on, it's important to show your process, not just the final product. People interested in your work will want to understand how you approach problems, how you explore and iterate on solutions, and how you incorporate user feedback. Include sketches, wireframes, prototypes, and any other artifacts that illustrate your process. Showcase your design thinking and your ability to solve complex problems.

Now, let's talk about storytelling. Each project in your portfolio should tell a story. This story should introduce the problem or challenge, your role in the project, how you approached the problem, the tools and methods you used, and the results you achieved. Remember, the best portfolios don't just show what you've done; they also reveal who you are as a designer.

Next up, it's essential to include user-centered design in your portfolio. As we've discussed before, understanding and meeting user needs is at the heart of UX design. Show how you conducted user research, used personas, created user journeys, and used other user-centered design techniques.

Don't forget to include some proof of your technical skills. This could be screenshots of your work in design software, snippets of code you've written, or a detailed explanation of how you conducted usability testing. This offers concrete proof of your technical proficiency, which can be particularly important for more technical roles.

One of the overlooked aspects of portfolio building is reflection. It's a great practice to include reflections on what you learned from each project and what you might do differently if you were to approach it again. This demonstrates a capacity for critical thinking and an appetite for continual learning, both highly desirable in a UX designer.

Accessibility and inclusive design are becoming increasingly important in UX design, and your portfolio should reflect this. Show examples of how you've considered accessibility in your designs, or how you've redesigned an interface to make it more inclusive.

Another key point is to keep your portfolio updated. As you grow and evolve as a designer, so should your portfolio. Regularly revisit and revise your portfolio to ensure it represents your current skills and abilities.

Finally, consider creating a digital portfolio. A digital portfolio is accessible to anyone with internet access and can be easily updated as you complete new projects. It also allows you to showcase any digital or interactive work in its native environment.

navigating the job market

Now, let's talk about how to navigate the job market, find the opportunities that suit your skills and interests, and land that dream UX design job.

Navigating the job market, whether you are a newbie to the field or a seasoned professional looking for a change, can be daunting. But fear not, the job market is bustling with opportunities for UX designers and with the right strategies, you can find a role that is the perfect fit.

First things first, networking. Yes, it's an overused term, but its importance cannot be overstated. A strong network can expose you to opportunities that may not be widely advertised, and can help you gain insights about potential employers. Attending industry conferences, joining professional associations, participating in online forums, and using platforms like LinkedIn can help you connect with fellow UX professionals.

Next, you should know how to tailor your application for each job. Ensure your resume and cover letter highlight the skills and experiences most relevant to the job description. Remember, hiring managers often review dozens of applications, so make yours stand out by clearly demonstrating how you meet the requirements of the job.

Speaking of resumes, as a UX designer, your

resume should be a testament to your design skills. It should be visually appealing, easy to read, and well-organized. Just like in your designs, ensure the information is user-centered; in this case, the user is the hiring manager.

While we're on the subject of job applications, remember your portfolio. You've spent time creating a stunning portfolio, make sure to use it. If possible, tailor your portfolio for each application. Highlight projects that are most similar to the work you would be doing in the job you're applying for.

Once your application is in, you need to prepare for the interviews. Typical UX design interviews may involve a mix of behavioral, situational, and technical questions. Some may also include a design exercise or a portfolio review. Prepare examples from your past experience that demonstrate your design process, problem-solving skills, and ability to collaborate with others.

But what about negotiating job offers, you might ask? That's an essential part of the process. Understand your value in the market. Research average salaries for similar roles in your area, consider the entire compensation package, not just the salary, and don't be afraid to negotiate.

Now, it's worth noting that the job market is not a one-size-fits-all scenario. There are various avenues available to UX designers, from full-time positions to contract work, freelancing, and even entrepreneurship. Each has its pros and cons, and what's right for you will depend on your personal circumstances, career goals, and risk tolerance.

continuous learning in ux

With technology changing at the speed of light, UX design trends, techniques, and tools are continually evolving. As such, the skill set of a UX designer today might look quite different a few years down the line. That's why continuous learning is not just a recommendation for UX designers—it's a necessity.

First off, let's consider the formal avenues for continuous learning. Many educational institutions and online platforms offer advanced courses in UX design, often with a focus on the latest tools and techniques. These structured learning environments can provide valuable opportunities to deepen your knowledge and expand your skill set. Some organizations even offer tuition reimbursement for job-related courses, so don't hesitate to explore this possibility.

Webinars and workshops are another excellent way to keep your skills up to date. They are often shorter than formal courses and can provide valuable insights into specific areas of UX design. Many of these are offered online, making it easy to fit them into your schedule.

Then, there's the whole wide world of books, blogs, and podcasts. These resources can provide a wealth of information on a variety of UX topics. Make a habit of reading industry-related articles, listen to UX podcasts during your commute, and keep a UX design book on your nightstand. This way, you'll constantly expose yourself to new ideas and perspectives.

Another way to ensure continuous learning is by attending industry conferences. Not only do these events offer informative sessions that can help you stay abreast of the latest trends and best practices, but they also provide invaluable networking opportunities. Meeting and exchanging ideas with other UX professionals can lead to a significant amount of learning and growth.

Of course, let's not forget the most hands-on method of learning—learning by doing. Every project you undertake is an opportunity to learn something new. Whether it's a challenging client requirement, a new user demographic, or an unfamiliar industry, each project can expand your knowledge and skills.

Feedback, as we discussed in a previous section, is another powerful learning tool. By seeking feedback from colleagues, clients, and users, you can gain insights into your strengths and areas for improvement. Remember, constructive criticism is not a personal attack; it's an opportunity for growth.

We also need to talk about learning from failure. It's a tough pill to swallow, but sometimes our designs don't work out as planned. When that happens, take a step back and analyze what went wrong. What could you have done differently? What can you learn from the experience? This kind of reflective learning can be immensely valuable in your development as a UX designer.

12 /
conclusion

recap of key learnings

FROM UNDERSTANDING its basic principles to navigating the fast-paced job market, we've traversed an expansive array of topics. As we approach the culmination of this exploratory journey, it's time to take a moment to reflect and recap some of the most pivotal learnings we've garnered along the way.

We embarked on our journey with the essentials: understanding what UX design is and why it matters. We learned that at its core, UX design is about enhancing user satisfaction by improving the usability, accessibility, and interaction between the user and the product. A successful UX design is one that aligns with the user's needs and expectations, making their interaction seamless, efficient, and enjoyable.

Diving deeper into the world of UX, we explored the crucial role of research in the design process. Understanding our users— their needs, behaviors, motivations—is pivotal in crafting designs that truly resonate with them. We learned that there are numerous research methods at our disposal, each with its own strengths and limitations. Combining qualitative and quantitative methods allows us to gain a comprehensive understanding of our users.

From research, we moved on to the art of creating personas and user journeys. These tools help us humanize our users, fostering empathy and understanding. We also delved into the importance of usability testing, reminding us that the design process is iterative and that user feedback is invaluable.

We talked extensively about effective communication, especially the importance of feedback. We discovered that utilizing feedback is not only about receiving it but also about giving it constructively and empathetically. It's a two-way street that requires patience, understanding, and a shared desire to improve the user experience.

Next, we entered the realm of future-proofing designs and the critical elements of data privacy and security. In an era where data is the new oil, we learned the importance of gaining user consent transparently and working towards minimizing design biases.

Keeping our focus on the future, we explored emerging technologies and their impact on UX design. We saw how technologies like AI, VR, and AR are pushing the boundaries of what's possible, and as UX professionals, we must be ready to adapt and evolve with these changes.

We also took a deep dive into the industry-standard tools, analyzing their pros and cons, and guiding you towards making an informed choice suitable for your project requirements. We further examined successful and failed designs, gleaning lessons and tips to guide our future endeavors.

The path to becoming a successful UX professional is not just about mastering skills and techniques. It involves building a strong portfolio, effectively navigating the job market, and most importantly, committing to continuous learning. The UX field is dynamic, and to stay relevant, we need to be agile learners, open to new ideas, and willing to adapt.

Before we wrap up this reflection, let's not forget the importance of networking and community. As we learned, being a part of the UX community can open doors to mentorship, learning opportunities, collaborations, and even job prospects. Engaging in dialogue with other UX professionals, sharing insights, and gaining different perspectives can be immensely enriching.

We've covered a lot of ground together, haven't we? It's been a journey of discovery, growth, and learning. Each section has built on the concepts from the previous ones, leading us to a more nuanced understanding of the field of UX design. But remember, our learning doesn't stop here. As we've often emphasized, the field of UX design is constantly evolving, and so should our knowledge.

the role of ux in shaping the future of technology

! In our previous sections, we've explored the expanse of user experience design, its evolving nature, and its profound impact on how we interact with technology. But what role does UX play in shaping the future of technology itself? In this section, we'll delve into the fascinating world where UX design and future technologies intersect, and how the former helps steer the course of the latter.

First, let's acknowledge an undeniable truth - technology is ceaselessly evolving, bringing in new possibilities and challenges alike. Every leap forward, be it in AI, AR, VR, IoT, or any other tech frontier, transforms how we interact with digital interfaces and how these interfaces serve us. Amidst this rapid evolution, UX design plays a critical role. It is UX that ensures that while we ride this wave of tech revolution, we do not lose sight of the humans who will use this technology.

To understand the role of UX in shaping technology's future, let's start with the most disruptive force in the digital world today - Artificial Intelligence. AI is transforming every sphere of technology, automating processes, providing insights, and creating personalized experiences. But without strategic UX design, AI interfaces could easily become confusing, overwhelming, or even downright creepy. As UX professionals, our role is to humanize these interactions, bringing in transparency, approachability, and relevance to AI-enabled experiences.

Consider AI-driven personalization, a key trend in modern UX. When done right, it feels like magic. When done poorly, it can feel invasive. A significant part of getting it right involves making complex algorithms understandable and controllable for everyday users. It is here that UX shines, translating technical complexity into simple, intuitive interfaces. Through thoughtful design, we can enable users to understand and control how their data is used, creating AI experiences that are not just smart, but also trusted and valued.

Next, let's shift our gaze towards Augmented Reality and Virtual Reality. AR and VR are opening up incredible new dimensions for human-computer interactions. We are moving from flat screens to three-dimensional, immersive experiences, a shift that demands a radical rethink of UX design principles. The challenge is to design interfaces that feel natural and intuitive in these immersive spaces, enabling users to navigate, interact, and achieve their goals seamlessly. As UX designers, we have a pivotal role in determining how these technologies mature and how they are adopted by mainstream users.

The Internet of Things is another frontier where UX is playing a critical role. As our homes, cities, and everyday objects get 'smart', the challenge is to design interactions that bring real value without adding unnecessary complexity. Good UX design can help create IoT solutions that are useful, usable, and delightful, helping this promising technology to reach its full potential.

As we look at these tech trends, it becomes clear that the future of technology is not just about new capabilities, but also about new experiences. And creating these experiences is precisely where UX design comes in.

But how do we, as UX professionals, equip ourselves for this future? It starts with embracing a mindset of continuous learning. As technologies evolve, so should our skills and perspectives. We should actively seek to understand new technologies, experiment with them, and imagine how they can enhance user experiences.

Another crucial aspect is collaboration. The future of technology is increasingly interdisciplinary, bringing together experts from diverse fields. As UX designers, we should embrace opportunities to collaborate with technologists, data scientists, psychologists, and other professionals, leveraging their expertise to create holistic, well-rounded experiences.

final thoughts and advice

As we reflect on our journey and look to the future, I'd like to share some final thoughts and advice, drawn from the wisdom we've gathered along the way. These are meant to serve as guiding principles as you continue your own journey in the ever-evolving field of UX design.

1. Keep Users at the Heart of Your Design Process

Remember, UX design is all about understanding and fulfilling users' needs and desires. The best design solutions emerge when we deeply empathize with our users and keep them at the heart of our design process. By doing so, we create digital experiences that resonate with our users on a human level, going beyond mere functionality to create truly delightful and meaningful interactions.

2. Never Stop Learning and Growing

In a field as dynamic as UX, continuous learning is key to staying relevant. New technologies, methodologies, and best practices emerge regularly. As UX professionals, we should be always curious, seeking to understand these new trends and exploring how they can enhance our design work. Whether it's learning about AI and AR, brushing up on behavioral psychology, or exploring new design tools, let's commit to lifelong learning.

3. Embrace Experimentation and Innovation

Don't be afraid to think outside the box and push the boundaries of conventional UX design. Remember, many of today's standard UX practices were once innovative ideas that someone dared to try. Experiment with different design approaches, iterate on your ideas, and be open to failures along the way. Every experiment, whether it succeeds or fails, is a stepping stone to a better design solution.

4. Collaboration is Key

UX design is a multidisciplinary field, bringing together insights from psychology, technology, art, and more. Collaboration with professionals from diverse disciplines not only enriches your design solutions but also helps you grow as a designer. Be open to different perspectives, leverage the expertise of your colleagues, and strive to create a synergistic work environment.

5. Advocate for Ethical and Inclusive Design

As UX professionals, we have a responsibility to advocate for ethical and inclusive design. We must ensure that our designs respect users' privacy, diversity, and well-being. Inclusion should not be an afterthought, but a fundamental aspect of our design process, ensuring that our digital experiences are accessible and meaningful for all users, regardless of their abilities, backgrounds, or contexts.

6. Stay Grounded in Your Purpose

Finally, amidst the whirlwind of design briefs, user testing, and iteration cycles, remember your purpose as a UX designer: to make technology more human, more meaningful, and more delightful. Stay grounded in this purpose. Let it guide your design decisions, inspire your creativity, and fuel your passion for UX design.

As this book closes, remember that your journey as a UX designer does not end here. In fact, it is just beginning. Each project, each interaction, and each user you encounter is a new opportunity to learn, grow, and make a difference through your design work. Carry the wisdom you've gleaned from these sections, add to it from your experiences, and forge your unique path in the vast, vibrant field of UX design.

appendices

glossary of ux terms

Having navigated our way through the wide and wonderful world of user experience, we've certainly encountered quite the collection of terms and jargon. But don't worry! In this section, we'll break down these terms and clarify their meanings. This way, you can easily refresh your memory and reinforce your understanding. So let's dive into our UX vocabulary!

1. User Experience (UX)

A broad term that encompasses a person's emotions, attitudes, and overall satisfaction when using a product, system, or service. It's not just about usability; it's also about how using the product makes someone feel.

2. User Interface (UI)

The elements of a product that the user interacts with directly. This includes buttons, forms, images, text, and any other controls a user might interact with.

3. Interaction Design (IxD)

A subset of UX that deals with the way users interact with products, systems, or services. This includes everything from how a button reacts when clicked, to how a user navigates through a website.

4. Usability

The extent to which a product can be used by specified users to achieve specified goals with effectiveness, efficiency, and satisfaction in a specified context of use. In simpler terms, it's about how easy and pleasant a product is to use.

5. Accessibility

The design of products, devices, services, or environments for people with disabilities. In the digital world, this means designing interfaces that can be used by everyone, regardless of their abilities.

6. Wireframe

A visual guide that represents the skeletal framework of a website or app. Wireframes are used in the planning stage of a project to establish the basic structure before any content or visual design is added.

7. Prototype

An early model or release of a product built to test a concept or process. In UX, prototypes are often used to

test the usability of an interface before the final product is developed.

8. Information Architecture (IA)

The organization and structure of a website, app, or other product. It involves determining how to arrange the parts of something to be understandable and navigable for users.

9. User Research

The process of understanding user behaviors, needs, and motivations through observation techniques, task analysis, and other feedback methodologies. It's a key component of UX design to ensure the end product will meet the needs of the user.

10. User Persona

A fictional character created to represent a user type that might use a site, brand, or product in a similar way. Personas are useful in considering the goals, desires, and limitations of brand buyers and users to help guide decisions about a service, product or interaction space.

ux checklist

As we inch towards the final sections of this book, I'd like to introduce a handy tool that can help you navigate the sea of UX design processes. We've all been there - you're in the midst of a project, it's crunch time, and the tasks at hand seem to blur into one big UX puzzle. That's when a simple UX checklist can come to the rescue, providing clarity, organization, and a sense of direction.

A UX checklist is a guide that helps ensure that all essential steps in the UX process are not only identified but also executed effectively. Let's break down some key aspects that could form part of your UX checklist:

1. Understanding Your User

Define User Persona: Start by defining your target user's persona - their needs, behaviors, and goals. Keep this persona at the heart of all design decisions.

Conduct User Research: Collect and analyze data about your users. Surveys, interviews, and observation are some methods you can use.

2. Competitor Analysis

Identify Your Competitors: Determine who your direct and indirect competitors are.

Analyze Their Products: Review their products, focusing on their design, strengths, weaknesses, and unique selling propositions.

3. Information Architecture

Create a Sitemap: Outline the structure of your website or application, defining how the pages and features will interconnect.

Draft User Flows: Illustrate the path a user might

take to accomplish tasks within your website or application.

4. Interaction Design

Sketch Wireframes: Create low-fidelity representations of each page to establish functionality and group relevant information together.

Develop Prototypes: Build interactive models of the final product to simulate user interactions.

5. Usability Testing

Plan Your Tests: Determine what aspects of your design you want to test, who your testers will be, and how you'll collect feedback.

Conduct Usability Tests: Carry out tests, observe user interactions, and take note of any difficulties they experience.

6. Visual Design

Select Color Schemes: Choose colors that align with your brand and support usability.

Determine Typography: Pick fonts that are legible and aesthetically pleasing, enhancing the overall user experience.

7. Content Strategy

Plan Content: Determine what type of content is needed and where it should be placed for maximum effectiveness.

Write Copy: Craft clear, concise, and engaging text that guides users through your site or application.

8. Review and Iteration

Gather Feedback: After the design is completed, gather feedback from stakeholders and users.

Iterate Design: Based on the feedback, make the necessary changes to your design.

Each project may require different aspects to be focused on, so feel free to customize this checklist to suit your needs.